S0-BTA-701

Masterpiece Sweaters

Masterpiece Sweaters

12 Dramatic New Designs

Janice Wright

Photographs by Mark Wright

Down East Books
Camden, Maine

Copyright © 1994 by Janice Wright
ISBN 0-89272-334-3
Library of Congress Catalog Number 94-71053
Book design by Dawn Peterson
Color Separations: Four Colour Imports, Louisville, Ky.
Printed and bound in Hong Kong at Everbest Printing

5   4   3   2   1

Down East Books / Camden, Maine

CONTENTS

ACKNOWLEDGMENTS

I would like to thank all my family and friends for their patience with this project, which involved lending back their sweaters for the year it took to write the instructions. Thank you, Lois, Mark, Amos, Hannah, Georgie, Meg, Susan, Lucille, Emily, Darragh, and Barbara.

Many thanks to the following people, whose contributions were invaluable in realizing this book: Mark Wright for his lovely photographs, Susan Ransome for her unparalleled skills in proofing the early manuscript, Karin Womer at Down East Books for meticulous final editing, Halcyon Blake and the staff at Halcyon Yarn for their help in organizing all the information on yarn equivalents (not to mention their wonderful yarn selections), Louis Carrier for his patient computerization of the charts, Marie Litterer for final renderings of the technical drawings, Harrisville Designs and Sharon Driscoll for generously contributing their beautiful yarns for a number of these projects. Thank you, also, to the models who gave so willingly of their time: Hannah Wright, Carey Friedman, Meg Stevens, Carol Wark, Lila Percy, Kathy Butner, Lois Wright, Andrea Tracy, Amos Wright, Sarah Robie, and Georgianna Wright.

INTRODUCTION: *A World of Inspiration*

The sweaters in this book were knitted for friends and family. They represent about five years of knitting. I'm not a professional knitwear designer, just a passionate knitter. My grandmother taught me to knit in my early teens. But knitting did not claim a big interest in my life until a friend gave me *Glorious Knits*, by Kaffe Fassett, in 1985. His unique approach to using yarn as a "fiber palette" really captured my imagination. I knit a couple of sweaters from that book, then my own design ideas began springing to mind faster than I could knit them.

I am an artist. I make paintings, pastels, and woodcuts focused on landscape. My landscapes are realistic, although they spring from a very abstract approach. Color, texture, and light in the natural world excite me. My paintings evolve into landscapes from working with these elements.

Plying multiple strands of yarn to create color, texture, and light in a knitted fabric appealed to me instantly on seeing Fassett's knitting. Up to that point, I was a casual collector of yarns. I had acquired a knitting machine to pursue an interest in intricate lace-knit garments, so I had a fair collection of lightweight yarns for combining into my own "custom" yarns.

All of the sweaters in this book may be knit either by hand or machine (except for the Seashells cardigan and Oak Leaves vest, which should be hand knit only). Four of the sweaters shown in the photographs I knit on a bulky-gauge knitting machine: Riotous Reindeer, the multicolor version of Sea Ducks, Victorian Firs, and Daylilies. The others I made by hand. I have included instructions for both methods for all designs except for the two mentioned above.

One key to the success of many of the sweaters in this book is the variety of colors or shades of yarns used. I hope that in addition to replicating my designs you will be inspired to create your own color blends and even your own design motifs. Please don't let the idea of blending yarns intimidate you; it's your "go ahead" to collect a wide variety of yarns. When you see a beautiful yarn, buy a skein and add it to your collection. That one skein may find its way into half-a-dozen sweaters! It is also a very economical approach to yarn purchases. Instead of going out and spending upward of a hundred dollars for one sweater, you can gradually build a yarn supply to draw from for each project. It is a great method for those of us who lead a life succinctly described as "creative poverty."

Oftentimes knitting friends tell me they lack the confidence to choose their own colors for a sweater. This always surprises me. We make color choices when we decorate our houses, when we plant our gardens, even when we prepare meals! Artists may be more aware of color—how it works or doesn't work—but you don't need any fancy color theory courses to understand color. I believe your own intuition about color and a keen sense of observation are all you need to use color effectively.

Train yourself to become a conscious observer. You need not go any further than your garden. Nature seems to make, then break, all the rules ever mentioned in color theory. All you have to do is to take note of what appeals to you. Then the joy of mixing yarns for an infinite variety of color will come naturally.

These twelve designs are inspired by many different sources. This is where conscious observation comes in again. I was fortunate in high school to have a wonderful, eccentric art teacher, Mrs. Ferguson. I will never forget her khaki green hair. More important, I will never forget her wild enthusiasm for art from around the world, art from ancient times to modern. It was the most broad-minded introduction to art one could hope for.

That enthusiasm for finding a bit of art wherever I go has served me well over the years. I am also fortunate to live on the northern edge of Casco Bay, and the influences of the Maine coast are evident in a couple of these sweaters. But even the Sea Ducks sweater, with its obvious marine wildlife influence, was actually inspired by a modern Peruvian rug I saw in an import store.

Chinese pottery motifs, Japanese kimono design, South American weavings, North American hooked rugs and quilts, European laces and embroideries, Scandinavian traditional knits, modern graphics from around the world—the list of influences is endless.

Keep a notebook in your bag when you go out and about. If you see something that really inspires you, make a quick sketch, jot down notes on colors. The sketches need not be fancy—the quickest cartoon will do. If I showed you my notebook, which I would be embarrassed to do, you would be surprised at the clumsiness of some of the sketches. It is amazing how humble little sketches can blossom into exciting sweaters.

WORKING WITH COLOR

Do you need baskets, boxes, and trunks full of yarn to knit some of these sweaters? If you are bent on faithful duplication of the originals, yes. But it is my hope that you will use the designs as a springboard for your own creativity and resourcefulness. Although some of the sweaters have elaborate shading, you can certainly simplify the colors into more basic color groups. The charts present the designs in simple colors, i.e., light pink, dark pink, apricot. You could easily and quite successfully substitute tweed or heather yarns for the more detailed blends. Take a look at the two versions of Sea Ducks (page 43); the multicolor version used a fair number of bulky weight tweeds rather than blends of finer yarns.

There are very detailed yarn lists in the back of the book for the sweaters knit with blended yarns (Seashells, Sea Ducks, Floral Tapestry, Garden Exotica, Floral Patchwork, and Oriental Motif). If you look over these lists, you will notice that certain colors and types of yarn appear in sweater after sweater. I guess they form my basic yarn palette. Each of us has favorite colors, so your basic yarn palette could be very different from mine.

Do not be intimidated by the thought of mixing your own yarns. The rules are really very simple. If you are blending yarns for a red flower, for example, gather up all your red yarns plus a few pinks (the pale end of the red scale) and some maroon (dark end of the red scale). Spread them out on the floor or table. Decide which end of the scale you want to work from, let's say the dark end. Take a couple of your darkest red and maroon, pull out a length of, say, one and a half yards. Break off the maroon, tie on (with a square knot) another dark red. Pull out a length of these two dark reds, say two yards. Break off one of the dark reds and add a medium red, pulling out another random length. Break off the dark red and add another medium red, pulling out a long random length — say, three yards. This progres-

sion of reds represents the body of your flower.

Now work toward the lighter end of the red scale. You can even introduce a patch of orange before you progress to the pinks. You might end your red progression with double pink to indicate the sunlit edge of a flower, perhaps a combination of mohair and pearl cotton. When you have finished the progression, there will be quite a pile of yarn at your feet or on your table. Wind it all up in a ball. I like to use a wool winder for this because then I can see the blendings of yarn, and I have the option of pulling yarn from the inside or outside of the "bun."

The rule here is to keep your progressions subtle, although a streak of complementary color is sometimes very striking. Remember, Nature loves to break rules. Try to keep your yarn combinations of a similar thickness. (If you have some very thin yarns, you can triple them.) Slight variations in thickness add textural interest, but drastic variations in thickness can distort the knitting. As you knit, if you find a color combination that does not suit you, break it off and go to the next. You'll probably work the discarded one in somewhere else. Don't worry too much about controlling the color progression. The element of surprise is the true joy in this kind of knitting. You might find that you can't put your knitting down. ("Just one more row . . . just one more row. . . .")

CHOOSING YOUR YARNS

The sweaters in this book are composed predominantly of wool yarns. Wool takes color and *keeps* color beautifully. Its resiliency allows it to keep its shape for many wearings over many years. I have not found cotton to be so reliable; it fades, and simply does not have the "life" inherent in wool. Since these sweaters represent a fair investment in time, I want them to last, and wool seems to do that best.

I do use mohair, cotton, rayon, and silk for the unique contributions each can make in a knitted design. Mohair provides a soft, fuzzy blending medium, muting color changes beautifully. Rayon, silk, and cotton can provide a luminous, soft sheen to yarn blends. Most of the yarns I purchase are sport weight or lighter, so when they are combined they knit up equivalent to a worsted weight or bulky yarn.

I love to haunt yarn stores for sales or closeouts. But mostly, I rely on Halcyon Yarn, a mail-order weaving and knitting supply business in Bath, Maine, that recently opened to retail customers. Their line of Victorian two-ply wool, mohair, and Harrisville Designs Shetland Style are the foundation for most of my sweaters. There are many such companies listed in the backs of knitting magazines. Their advantage is that they offer an incredible variety of quality yarns. Quality is important when you invest so much time in a sweater. For a modest charge, most of the mail-order companies will send you samples of their yarns, with periodic updates throughout the year. Of course, if you are fortunate enough to live near a well-stocked yarn store, you will be able to see and handle the actual skeins of yarn, and you won't have to wait for mail-order delivery. Between your own local stores and the mail-order suppliers, you will have extensive choices for creating unique sweaters.

Although I usually buy yarns that are sport weight or lighter, I also have a fair supply of worsted weight and bulky yarns. When deciding on the color scheme of a particular sweater, I usually need to purchase extra yarns for the background and perhaps a few extra colors for the motifs. The leftovers from these yarns are added to my boxes for a future design.

Harrisville Designs' Shetland Style and Tweeds in sport weight and 2-ply; Halcyon Yarn's sport weight Victorian, mohairs, pearl cottons, and silks; Jagger Spun Maine Line 2/8s; Reynolds Kitten, and novelty blends of cottons, rayons, cotton chenille, angora, and alpaca are combined in the blended-yarn sweaters. These can all be

---

Yarn Combinations that Yield Comparable Gauges

Most of the sweaters using blended yarns have a gauge of 3¾ to 4 stitches per inch. The general guidelines I follow for combining yarns to knit this gauge are as follows:

- 3 strands of fingering weight yarns
- 2 strands of sport weight yarns
- 1 strand sport weight with 1 strand mohair
- 2 strands fingering weight yarns with 1 strand sport weight
- 1 strand fingering weight with 1 strand worsted weight
- 2 strands fingering weight single-ply with 1 strand sport weight
- 1 strand worsted weight or lighter novelty yarns can be combined with 1 strand fingering weight yarn
- single strand of bulky weight

Converting Skein Information to Yards per Pound

Yarns are now available in such a wide variety of weights per ball that it is extremely useful to know how to convert the yards-per-skein information usually found on the label to yards-per-pound and use that figure to compare various skeins of yarn. To do this, divide the number of yards by the number of ounces in the skein to give the number of yards per ounce. Then multiply this total by 16 (16 oz = 1 lb) to give the number of yards per pound.

Many international yarns give weights in grams, so you will first have to convert grams to ounces: 50 grams = 1.75 ounces; 100 grams = 3.5 ounces.

(Example: Lopi yarn has 110 yards per skein, 100 grams per skein. 110 yards ÷ 3.5 ounces = approximately 33 yards per ounce. 33 x 16 = 528 yards per pound. On the Yarn Size Specifications table below, this puts Lopi in the bulky weight category, meaning that it can be used successfully alongside blended yarns or as a substitute for blended yarns.)

Labels on most foreign yarns do not list *meters* per skein, but if you should happen to encounter one that does, 1 meter = 1.09 yards.

doubled, even tripled, to give you an infinite choice of colors.

Some knitters will not have the patience to collect and blend their own yarns (or the inclination to fill their houses with trunks full of yarn). For those knitters, exciting possibilities still exist. Just look for heavy weight yarns that will knit up to the gauge of the sweater you've chosen. Many beautiful yarns are available for large-gauge knitting. In the individual sweater instructions I've provided information on overall weight of the sweater, plus how that weight is broken down proportionally for each color group. Most skeins of knitting yarn come with basic gauge

and weight information on their tags. Use this information to decide whether a particular yarn is an appropriate substitute and how much you will need to purchase. (See "Converting Skein Information to Yards per Pound" above.)

How do you know whether a yarn fits into the categories of fingering, sport, worsted, or bulky weight? The yarn industry uses a system of yards-per-pound to classify yarns. In the following chart, you will notice that each category has a range for gauge, needles, and yards per pound. As some yarns end up straddling these categories, needle size will play a substantial role in what your final gauge will be. Wool yarns are

Yarn Size Specifications

Yarn Size	Symbol	WPI	Approx. Gauge	Needle Size	Est. Yards/Pound
Fingering Weight	F	16 WPI	7 st/inch	1–3	1700–2300 yds/lb
Sport Weight	S	14 WPI	5½ to 6½ st/inch	4–6	1200–1600 yds/lb
Worsted Weight	W	12 WPI	4 to 5 st/inch	7–9	850–1100 yds/lb
Bulky Weight	B	9 WPI	3 to 3½ st/inch	10–11	500–900 yds/lb

Chart reprinted courtesy of Priscilla Gibson-Roberts, *Knitter's* magazine very flexible, so you will find that you can use yarns with reasonable variation in yards per pound together in the same sweater. Cottons, silks, and rayons that knit up to the same *gauge* as wool will have very different yards per pound. To estimate equivalent yarns of different fibers (or the same fiber with different densities, such as a heavy single-ply tweed vs. a combination of two or three fine yarns), it is better to use wraps per inch.

In the table on page 14, WPI stands for wraps per inch. This is a technique long used by weavers to estimate setts for weaving. It is also a useful measurement for knitters in *estimating* yarn size and gauge, especially when buying yarns from a weaving supply company for knitting. (For example, increasing numbers of knitters are discovering the extensive and consistent range of colors available from Harrisville Designs, which has served weavers for years.)

Weaving yarns often come with yards-per-pound and WPI information. You can use that information with this chart to estimate a particular yarn size, and thus determine how you can use it for custom blending or substituting as described above.

To find your own WPI, wrap the yarn, or yarn combinations you are considering, around a ruler for one inch. Actually it is best to wrap yarn for three or four inches and take an average of the wraps (by dividing number of wraps by three or four). Be careful not to stretch the yarn(s). Wrap so the yarn(s) allow no open space but do not overlap. For yarn combinations, twist the yarns together *loosely* before you wrap so they lie as one yarn and not as multiple strands. Count the number of wraps, check your count against the table on page 14, and you will be able to approximate yarn size and gauge.

All this information gives you a starting point for deciding how a particular yarn could be used. It is still imperative that you knit sample swatches to determine the actual knitting gauge of the yarn or yarn combination you want to use. The needle size and your personal knitting style will play a big role in the tension gauge. (I am a loose knitter and achieve a bulky gauge on size 8 and 9 needles, though according to the chart, I should be using size 10 needles.) You will have to experiment to come up with the right combination of yarns and needles. It won't be long before you develop an intuitive sense and by the look and feel of a yarn will know how to use it. This kind of knitting is a creative adventure — an antidote to TV and boredom. Have fun — experiment!

The detailed yarn lists for the sweaters that were made with many yarn combinations could be daunting to some knitters. That is why they are in the back of the book (beginning on page 115). Use the photographs and basic yarn information given in the sweater instructions to transform a sweater into *your own* unique expression. I would love to get snapshots of your efforts!

Estimating Yardage Needed to Make a Long-Sleeved Knitted Garment

| | Children's Sizes | | | | Wmn's Med. | Wmn's Lg. | Wmn's X–Lg. | |
	2	4	8	14	Men's Sm.	Men's Med.	Men's Lg.	Men's X–Lg.
Bulky	350	400	650	825	1000	1100	1200	1400
Worsted	420	500	800	950	1150	1250	1450	1700
Sport	500	600	950	1100	1400	1600	1800	2000
Fingering	690	830	1100	1400	1727	1950	2100	2300

Courtesy of Halcyon Yarn.

SPECIAL TECHNIQUES

I feel a real resistance to giving detailed instructions for knitting. My mother will roll her eyes when she reads this, but I do not knit using any instructions other than the basic chart I prepare for each design. I am the kind of person who opens a sewing pattern and promptly throws out the directions. But a number of knitting friends have convinced me that some of the methods used in these sweaters are a unique fusion of hand and machine techniques and require explanation.

The first special techniques I'll discuss evolved from substituting decorative borders for conventional ribbing. I have never liked knitting ribbing by hand or by machine. When knitting ribbing by hand, I can never get it tight enough to look nice, and ribbing beds on knitting machines are the most intimidating pieces of machinery I have ever met.

A few years ago I was working on a sweater inspired by a traditional quilt design. It seemed logical to follow the quilt theme through and use geometric borders in place of conventional ribbing. It has become a basic component of my sweater designs. Veteran knitters of Norwegian sweaters will be familiar with the use of borders in lieu of ribbing. The difference in these sweaters is that the borders are knit after the main body pieces are complete.

With simple knitting machines, one is taught how to "hang hems" on knitted pieces. The methods for hanging hems involve casting on with waste yarn and a pull cord. The same basic method is used for attaching decorative borders.

I also use short rows to shape the shoulders and neck openings. In this section I will explain hanging hems and short-row shaping in detail, so the individual sweater instructions can remain simple.

In addition to discussing the particular techniques for decorative borders, I will touch briefly on the importance of weaving in yarn tails and blocking individual sweater pieces, and on the use of circular needles and care of wool sweaters.

I will assume that you are already familiar with most of the basic knitting and assembly techniques for knitting sweaters. If you are not experienced with multiple-color knitting, either Fair Isle or intarsia, there are dozens of excellent how-to books available in bookstores and libraries. Also, most yarn stores offer classes and friendly advice for new knitters.

Cast-On and Cast-Off Techniques

The decorative borders on the sweaters in this book call for a different approach to casting on than is usual with sweaters with ribbing. By using either a simple or invisible cast-on for sweaters with one main color in the cast-on row, or a cast-on with waste yarn and pull cord for the intarsia designs, one is able to go back after the front and back of the sweater have been sewn together, pick up all the stitches around the bottom, and knit seamless decorative borders. Since most of the borders have knitted facings, making them two layers thick, doing away with side seams in the hip area is desirable for most of us! The pull cord with waste yarn technique also gives a foundation for beginning the intarsia designs without a single-color cast-on row.

Very often as I designed the sweaters, I worked out the border designs only after the rest of the sweater was complete. It was necessary to see the impact of the design in the body and sleeves before adding the complementary borders. (This is analogous to choosing a frame to complement a piece of artwork rather than choosing the frame first and looking for artwork to fill it.) By using the technique described below, I had easy access to the first row of stitches.

Pull cord and waste yarn cast-off are often used in both Fair Isle and intarsia sweaters to knit off the shoulders and necks. This allows for the grafting of smooth, seamless shoulders (page 19).

CAST-ON WITH PULL CORD AND WASTE YARN

Since most machine knitters learn this very basic technique when they begin to use their machines, the following description will be directed to hand knitters.

Waste yarn: Use inexpensive wool or acrylic yarn in sport or worsted weight. I usually buy a couple of skeins in nondescript, ugly colors so I won't be tempted to save them.

Pull cord: The purpose of the pull cord is to allow you to pull off the waste knitting after you have picked up your main-yarn stitches. This must be a very smooth fiber. Machine knitters use a nylon cord that comes with their machines. It is usually quite thin and *very* strong. You may substitute pearl cottons, or cotton or rayon cord in sport or lighter weight. Use a light color that will not "bleed" when you wash and block your sweater pieces.

For waste yarn cast-on: Using the simplest cast-on method you know, and the needles indicated for knitting the main body of the sweater, cast on the required number of stitches with waste yarn.

Knit several rows. (You may want to work these rows in garter stitch to prevent rolling, but it is not strictly necessary.)

Break off the waste yarn and knit one row using the pull cord. Do not bother to secure the tails of pull cord and waste yarn.

Now you are ready to attach the main yarns and begin following the pattern chart.

When you have completed your sweater pieces and have sewn up the side seams, pick up

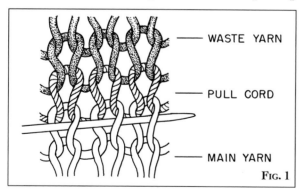

WASTE YARN

PULL CORD

MAIN YARN

FIG. 1

the stitches of the first row of main yarn(s), as shown in Figure 1. Use a tapestry needle to loosen the first couple of pull cord stitches. Since they are knit with a smooth yarn, they sometimes tighten on the edge, making them difficult to remove. If you have a tendency to knit tightly, you may have to snip the pull cord in several places to remove it.

Pull gently but firmly until the waste yarn is released.

Now you are ready to proceed with the decorative border.

CAST-OFF WITH PULL CORD AND WASTE YARN

After completing shoulder and neck shaping, I generally like to keep the final rows of stitches on hold rather than binding them off, so I can later graft the front and back shoulders together [Figure 5] and pick up the neck stitches for knitting the collar bands. For a small number of stitches—e.g., the shoulder stitches of the vests— you could just put the stitches on stitch holders or draw a piece of yarn through them with a tapestry needle, but generally speaking, if the knitting is going to sit around for a while, the pull cord/ waste yarn cast off is a lot more secure. It holds the shape and gauge of the last row of knitting, making the grafting and picking up of stitches easier later on.

Simply knit 1 row with pull cord, then several rows with waste yarn after the shaping of the piece is complete. Leave a tail of waste yarn to pull through the last row of waste yarn stitches with a tapestry needle. The pull cord and waste yarn are easily unraveled after grafting or picking up stitches.

SIMPLE CAST-ON AND INVISIBLE CAST-ON

You can also use a simple cast-on or invisible cast-on for the first row of knitting. I generally reserve these methods for sweaters that have one color in the cast-on row. Some people find it difficult to control and knit the first row of a simple cast-on, because the loops slip and pull. So I have included the invisible cast-on to give you a choice of methods.

Simple cast-on: Make a slip knot for the initial stitch. Place the slip knot on your needle and hold needle and slip knot in right hand.

Wrap the working end of the yarn around the left thumb and hold it in the left palm.

Put the needle through the yarn behind the thumb [Figure 2]. With the needle, lift and slide the new stitch next to the slip knot on the needle. Pull the working end of the yarn gently to secure the new stitch.

Repeat until you have the required number of stitches.

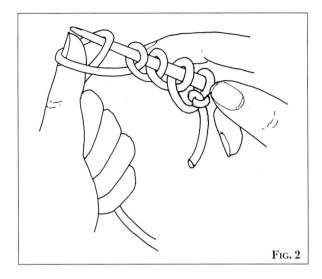

FIG. 2

Invisible cast-on: Take a length of waste yarn (in the same weight as the working yarn) and knot it together with the working yarn. Hold needle and knot in your right hand. Maintain tension in both yarns with your left hand. (Note: Some knitters may feel more comfortable if they secure the working yarn to the needle with a slip knot.)

Do a *yarn over* with the working yarn in front of the waste strand [Figure 3].

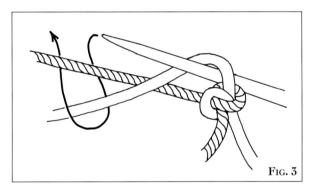

FIG. 3

Pivot the yarns, holding the waste yarn taut, and *yarn over* with the working yarn in back of the waste yarn [Figure 4].

Each *yarn over* creates a stitch. Continue mak-

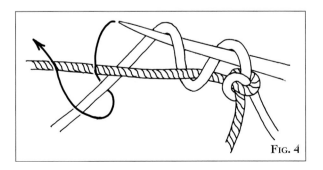

FIG. 4

ing alternate *yarn overs* for the required number of stitches.

To begin knitting, twist the working yarn around the waste strand for the first stitch, and work across, knitting into the front of all the loops.

Do not remove the waste yarn until you are ready to pick up this first row of loops for knitting the decorative borders.

Invisible Grafting

Invisible grafting (Figure 5) allows you to join sweater pieces with a smooth seam that won't interrupt designs that pass over the shoulders from front to back. It is *not* a good technique to use on loosely knit garments or with heavy yarns because the knitting can easily lose its shape on the shoulder.

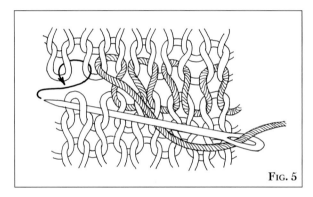

FIG. 5

Decorative Borders, Cuffs, and Neckbands

The decorative borders are knit after main sweater pieces are finished. This allows you to change borders if you want, and to knit seamless borders. They are usually knit on smaller needles than the body of the sweater, and sometimes on fewer stitches, so they will hold their shape.

Borders are finished off in a variety of ways — some with facings, some with rolled edges. It is best to knit the facings in a lighter weight yarn to reduce bulk. The borders with linings (facings) all have one or two rows of reverse stockinette stitch, which creates a row of purl stitches on the right side of the knitting that allows the border to fold neatly for the hem lining.

For machine knitters: To work the reverse stockinette stitch, use a garter bar to remove the knitting from the machine, turn, and rehang for the number of rows indicated on the chart. When the reverse rows are completed, use the garter bar to remove the knitting, turn, and rehang for knitting the lining of the decorative band.

If you do not have a garter bar, you can remove the knitting with a size 1 or 2, 24-inch circular needle, turn, and rehang. This is obviously not as efficient, but it works just as well and is a lot cheaper than investing in a garter bar.

FINISHING THE HEM ON BORDERS

For hand knitters: End the lining with a knit row and keep the stitches on the knitting needle. Use a tapestry needle to sew the first stitch to the very edge of the first row of border stitches. (This is usually knit in a contrast color, so it is easy to find.) Keep working across stitches, removing and sewing one stitch from the needle to its fellow on the first row of the border [Figure 6]. You can also use a simple loose cast-off and then sew the cast-off edge to the first row of the border. This is slightly more bulky but is quite acceptable and easy to do.

For machine knitters: After knitting the bor-

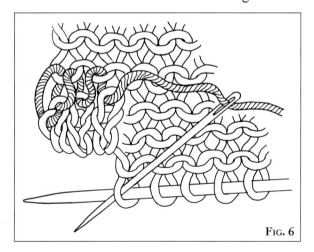

FIG. 6

der and lining, bring up the first row of border stitches and hang on the needles. Turn the tension dial 2 notches higher and knit one row with the carriage. Cast off with a tapestry needle.

Short-Row Shaping of Necklines and Shoulders

Shaping the neck and shoulders with short rows is a basic technique used by machine knitters that is gaining in popularity with hand knitters — for good reason. The technique is very useful in making tidy, smooth finishing for shoulder details and knitting on collar bands. It is especially helpful at the neck because it eliminates the need to pick up stitches from a cast-off edge, which I have always found difficult to do without leaving holes and a generally uneven looking pick-up row. With bulky yarns, short-row shaping also eliminates extra bulk at the neck.

The method is actually quite simple, although it may not seem so on first reading. With the technique decribed in great detail here, the general instructions for each sweater can be much less complicated. The individual pattern instructions will read, "Shape neck and shoulders using short rows."

SHORT ROWS FOR HAND KNITTERS

It might be very helpful to those of you who have not previously used short-row shaping of necks and shoulders to knit a practice piece as you read through the following directions. The sample chart is worked over 50 stitches, making it a scaled-down version with fewer stitches and rows than in an actual sweater, but the basic steps are the same.

Cast on 50 stitches with some spare yarn and knit about 6 rows, just enough so your sample

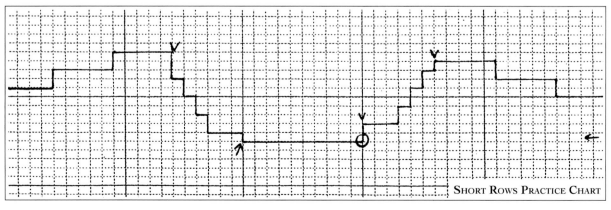

SHORT ROWS PRACTICE CHART

isn't rolling up as you try the short-row shaping—several rows of garter stitch will absolutely prevent your sample from rolling.

Generally speaking, the neck shaping on the pullover sweaters in this book starts before the shoulder shaping. When you reach the first row of the neckline (indicated by the arrow on the right-hand side of the practice chart), work across the stitches to the first "step" in the chart, marked in bold outline. This should be a two-row "step"—circled on our practice chart. This first "step"

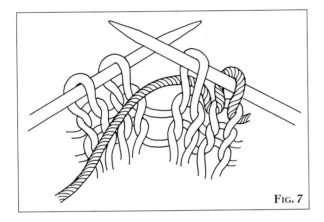

FIG. 7

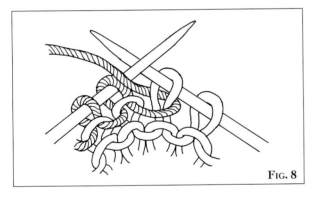

FIG. 8

usually occurs on a knit row, but not always. Shaping can happen on knit or purl rows; it makes no difference.

Before turning to work the next short row, slip the first stitch on the left needle purlwise [Figure 7]. Bring the yarn to the right side of the work, then slip the stitch back to the left needle. Turn the knitting and return the yarn to the working side [Figure 8]. Wrapping the yarn around the unworked stitch prevents gaps or holes from forming at the turn. Mark this turn with a contrasting yarn marker (indicated on the practice chart as V). Proceed back across the chart.

Keep working up the chart, knitting only the stitches that fall within the bold outline of the neck shaping, slipping stitches and wrapping yarn for each short row. (On the practice chart, you will knit 2 rows of 20 stitches, 2 rows of 17 stitches, and 1 row of 16 stitches.)

Now you have reached the first row of shoulder shaping. As you work back across this row, you will leave the stitches outside the bold outline unworked (4 stitches on the sample).

Slip the first stitch from the left needle purlwise. Bring the yarn forward, slip the stitch back to the left needle. Turn the work, bring the yarn to working position, and proceed back across the chart. You are now working neck shaping and shoulder shaping simultaneously.

When the last row of the right-hand side of the chart is worked, place a contrasting yarn marker to show the division between shoulder and neck stitches (indicated on the practice chart by V).

Knit one final row of shoulder stitches. This row is not shown on the charts (it is not really possible to include it). On the actual sweater patterns, just repeat the color sequence of the stitches already on the needles.

Place the shoulder stitches on a stitch holder, or cast off with a pull cord and waste yarn, or do a regular cast-off. Each pattern will indicate the appropriate method.

To continue neck shaping on the left side of the chart, transfer the short-row stitches of the neckline (between yarn markers) and the center neck stitches to your right-hand needle. (In our practice piece, this is 6 short-row stitches plus 10 center neck stitches.) Attach the yarn and follow the chart across the row from right to left (from the middle arrow to the left edge on the practice chart).

The shaping and turning of short rows is simply the reverse of the shaping you did on the first shoulder. Don't forget to wrap your stitches when you turn, to prevent holes.

When the shoulder shaping is complete, use a marker to separate shoulder from neck stitches, and work one last row across the shoulder stitches. Again, this will not be indicated on the chart, so just repeat color changes as they come up on the needles.

Work off the shoulder stitches in the same method as used on the other shoulder.

To Adapt Short-Row Shaping for Deeper Necklines

A deeper shaped neckline has more rows without short-row shaping. When working the final row of the neck edge, pick up stitches along the edge of these rows as you would on a traditional bound-off edge. Allow approximately 4 stitches per 5 rows, as you generally knit fewer stitches per inch than rows per inch.

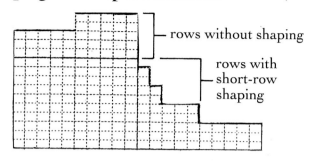

— rows without shaping

rows with — short-row shaping

Go back and work one more row across all the neck stitches. Work off the neck stitches onto a pull cord and waste yarn or place on a stitch holder.

You have completed the neck and shoulder shaping! The shoulder and neck stitches are separated into three sections, and you are ready to graft shoulders and knit the decorative neckbands.

SHORT-ROWS FOR MACHINE KNITTERS

We will use the same sample chart on page 20 to practice short-row shaping for machine knitters. If you are not already familiar with using short rows to shape the necks of pullovers, try following along here with a sample knit in waste yarn.

The individual pattern instructions will read: "Shape neck and shoulders with short rows." The neckline shaping on the pullover sweaters in this book begins before the shoulder shaping. When you reach the first row of the neckline (indicated by the arrow on the right-hand side of the practice chart), you are ready to begin short-row shaping. This should be a two-row "step"—circled on our practice chart. This first "step" can occur on the right- or left-hand side of the chart. If it is on the right side of the chart, the carriage is on the right side of the machine; if the first "step" is on the left side of the chart, the carriage is on the left side of the machine. If you have to knit an extra row to get the carriage to the correct side, do so; it won't make any appreciable difference in the sweater.

The practice chart is worked over 50 needles, making it a scaled-down version with fewer stitches and rows than in the actual sweaters.

Using waste yarn, cast on with any simple cast-on method over 50 needles and knit several rows, ending with the carriage on the right. Put carriage levers in hold position (abbreviated in the following instructions as HP).

Look at the chart. All needles to the left of the first 2-row "step" in bold outline on the neck (circled on the practice chart) are pulled to HP.

Move the carriage from right to left. Wrap the yarn under the first needle in HP next to the needles in working position [Figure 9]. This wrapping prevents holes from forming, so don't forget to wrap these needles between passes with the carriage.

Move the carriage from left to right.

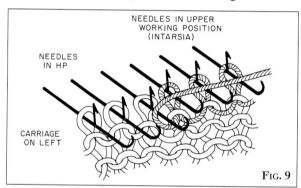

NEEDLES IN UPPER WORKING POSITION (INTARSIA)

NEEDLES IN HP

CARRIAGE ON LEFT

FIG. 9

Continue following the chart, pulling the needle(s) indicated in bold outline to HP (on the practice chart this is 3 needles and 1 needle). Wrap needles as above (from * to *).

When you reach the row where shoulder shaping begins, pull the shoulder-edge needles to HP (4 needles on the practice chart). Move the carriage from left to right, wrap the needle as described above. Pull needle indicated on the neck edge to HP.

Continue following chart, pulling needle(s) indicated in bold outline to HP (for the practice piece, this is 1 needle on the neck edge twice, 4 needles on the shoulder edge once).

The right-hand side of the chart is now completed.

Push all shoulder needles back to working position and knit 1 more row *on shoulder needles only*. If there are color changes on the chart you are working, repeat the color changes of the last row knit.

Knit off the shoulder needles using pull cord and waste yarn.

To continue shaping of shoulder and neck on the left side of the chart, push all needles on the left side (from the middle arrow on the practice chart) back to working position. Center neck and right neck needles remain in HP.

Attach yarn, carriage on the right. Knit 1 row from right to left.

Pull needles indicated in bold outline on neck edge to HP (3 on the practice chart).

Knit 1 row, wrap needle as described above.

Continue to follow the left side of the chart, pulling needles indicated in bold outline for neck and shoulder shaping as you come to them. Don't forget to wrap your needles.

When shaping is complete, push all the shoulder needles back to working position and knit 1 row. In actual sweater knitting, repeat the color changes of the last row.

Knit off the shoulder needles onto pull cord and waste yarn.

Push all neck needles back to working position and knit 1 last row. Knit off onto pull cord and waste yarn.

You have completed the neck and shoulder shaping. The shoulder and neck needles are separated into three sections, ready for grafting, or assembly by machine, and working of the decorative collar band.

Notes on Basic Color Knitting Techniques

When you leafed through this book, you probably noticed that color, and lots of it, is the theme for these sweaters. The techniques for getting that color into the sweaters are intarsia and Fair Isle, sometimes a combination of both. The design dictates whether one uses Fair Isle or intarsia technique in a given sweater.

Intarsia is used when a design changes color at least once across a row and the yarns not in use are *not* carried across the back of the work. The yarns are twisted, or crossed, when changing colors. As you follow across the chart, drop the working yarn over the new yarn as you change colors. Bring up the new working yarn from under the old working yarn. This twists the yarns and prevents holes from forming. Intarsia is used when the sweater design uses relatively large motifs rather than small repeat patterns—in Floral Tapestry, Daylilies, and Riotous Reindeer, for example. It is also used in repeat patterns when the pattern has large blocks of color, such as in the Sea Ducks and Interlocking Fishes designs.

Fair Isle technique is used when two or more yarns are used repeatedly across a row and the yarn not being worked is carried across the back until it is needed. The resulting knitted fabric is thicker than an intarsia knit because of the carried strands. Fair Isle is used for the repeating patterns used in the Victorian Firs and Oriental Motif sweaters and on a majority of the decorative collars, cuffs, and lower bands.

WEAVING IN "TAILS" ON COLOR KNITTING

When using many colors in a sweater, one ends up with dozens of beginning and ending yarn tails that must be secured. I cannot stress enough how important it will be in some of these sweaters to *weave in the tails as you are knitting them*. It is a daunting task to leave for later, but is quite simple to do as the knitting progresses. Check every few rows to make sure you haven't forgotten to weave in any tails. If you missed some, use a tapestry needle to weave them in back of the bars between stitches, or secure them with a half hitch, as described below.

Whenever possible, weave tails into stitches of the same or similar color.

For Hand Knitters

The technique for weaving in tails is basically the same as knitting in floating yarns on the back of the fabric in Fair Isle.

When starting a new color, be it at the beginning of a new row or in mid-row, break off about a 3-inch tail on the old yarn and hold it together with a like amount of tail on the new yarn as you knit the first stitch of new color.

After knitting the first stitch in the new color, take both tails and lay them over the working yarn. Work the next stitch.

Now insert the needle for the next stitch and bring the yarn tails back up and across the working yarn, then wrap, and work the next stitch. [Figure 10.]

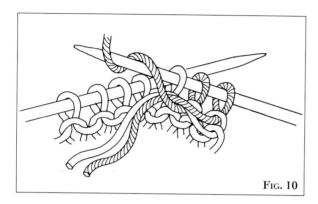

FIG. 10

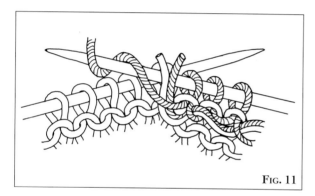

FIG. 11

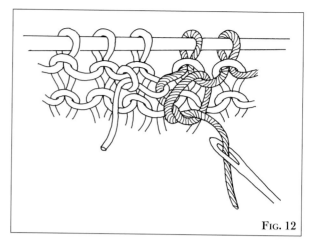

FIG. 12

Repeat this weaving-in for 4 or 5 stitches. [Figure 11.]

If the yarns are very bulky, or the contrast is very great between color changes, it may be desirable to weave in the tails separately. To do this and not leave holes at the change of color, knit the first stitch of new color, then twist the tail of the new color with the old-color tail, just as you do when twisting yarns for color changes in intarsia knitting. Weave in the new-color tail as described above. When you work back across the next row, pick up the old-color tail and weave it in. This way, each tail is woven in among stitches of the same color.

In sweaters with high contrast of colors, or too few stitches for a color to be knit back on itself, use a tapestry needle to secure the tails of beginning and ending yarns with a half hitch on

the "bar" of an adjoining stitch from the previous row [Figure 12].

If you are using pearl cottons or silks, it is always best to secure tails with tapestry needle half-hitch knots or square knots. Since pearl cotton and silk are smooth fibers, the ends can easily work their way out when the tails are simply woven in.

For Machine Knitters

Have a good supply of wooden clothes pins handy, plus a tapestry needle.

When starting a new color, whether at the beginning of a new row or in the middle of a row, clip a clothes pin to the tail of the new yarn. Lay the yarn over the needles indicated on the chart, with the pinned tail hanging down 3 to 4 inches. After you have laid the rest of your yarns across the needles and have knit the row, bring the yarn tail up and pass it over and under every other needle, either to the right or to the left, 3 or 4 times. It is best to weave the colors back on themselves if possible, so they won't show through on the right side.

Keep the clothes pin on the tail. Push the woven yarn *behind* the latches of the needles so it will knit invisibly on the next row [Figure 13]. If you don't push the yarn behind the latches, it will "jump" to the front of the knitting!

This technique works equally well for the beginning and ending tails.

In sweaters with high color contrast or too few stitches for a color to be knit back on itself, use a tapestry needle to secure the tails of beginning and ending yarns with a half hitch on the

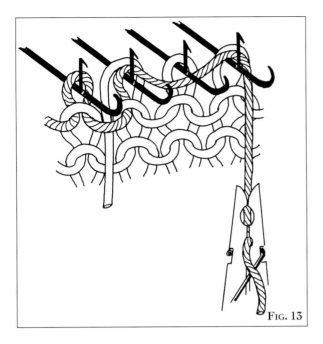

FIG. 13

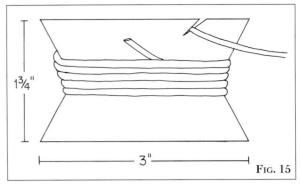

FIG. 15

"bar" of an adjoining stitch from the previous row [Figure 14]. If you are using pearl cottons or silks, secure all tails with the tapestry needle half-hitch knots or square knots so the tail of these smooth yarns will not work their way loose, as can happen when the tails are simply woven in.

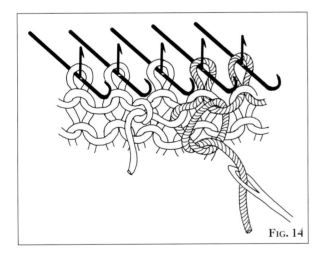

FIG. 14

HANDLING MULTIPLE STRANDS OF YARN

In intarsia sweaters, it is common to wrap yarn on bobbins. This is desirable for machine intarsia because the weight of the bobbins helps maintain yarn tension. You can fashion you own bobbins from heavy cardboard (not corrugated). See Figure 15 for dimensions. When blending yarns, handle each 2- or 3-strand combination as a "single" yarn, i.e., wind them together on the same bobbin.

For hand knitting with various lengths of yarn, I prefer to just let the yarn hang. This is fine for 1- to 4-yard lengths. They are easily untangled every few rows by gently shaking and combing your fingers through the yarns. For greater lengths, you can wrap "butterflies" as illustrated in Figure 16. Butterflies also work fine for machine intarsia.

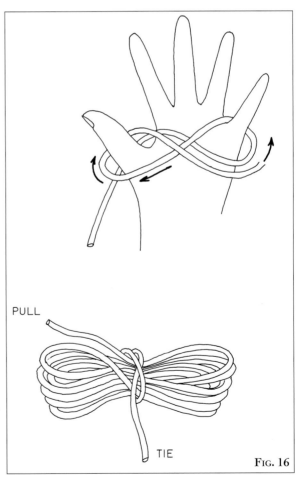

PULL

TIE

FIG. 16

Knitting a Tension Gauge

Please, please, please knit a tension gauge swatch before starting any of these projects, so you will be assured of getting the correct proportions in the size you choose. Everyone knits at a slightly different tension, so the needle sizes and machine tension setting are only suggestions. You may have to try different size needles or machine settings to come up with the correct gauge.

Make sure the swatch will measure 4 inches square. If the desired gauge is 16 stitches and 20 rows for 4 inches, knit a swatch of at least 24 stitches and 30 rows. This gives you a much more accurate gauge, especially when using multiple-blend yarns.

Needles

I like to use circular needles, even though the bodies of these sweaters are not knit in the round. A circular needle allows one to hold a fair amount of knitting comfortably in one's lap, and to be able to knit in armchairs or other somewhat confined spaces. They are also used for knitting the decorative borders on the lower edge of sweaters, which *are* worked in the round.

Sets of double-pointed needles can be used to knit the cuffs and smaller neckbands in the round.

Following the Charts

Although these sweaters appear to be complicated, they are not that difficult to knit. They do require reading the charts row by row. This is much easier to accomplish if you lay a clear plastic ruler on the chart, one row above the row you are working. I suggest a clear plastic ruler so you can keep an eye on what is coming up in the next row. Sometimes a yarn will be picked up several stitches ahead of where it was dropped on the previous row. It is a good idea to anticipate this and carry the yarn to where you will need it, by weaving in, just as you do for long floats in Fair Isle knitting.

Increases and Decreases

Increases and decreases are clearly marked on the charts. They are usually referred to very briefly in the written instructions. I generally use full-fashion increases or decreases for shaping sleeves, armholes, and neck openings for cardigans and vests. "Full fashion" simply means making increases or decreases on the second stitch in from the edge.

When an increase or decrease is indicated at the beginning of a row, knit the first stitch, then make your increase or decrease on the second stitch. The same applies for increases or decreases that occur at the end of the row: Knit to within the last 2 or 3 stitches, work the increase or decrease on the second-to-last stitch, then work the edge stitch.

For machine knitters: Full-fashion increases are easily accomplished by using the two-pronged transfer tool. Lift off the 2 edge stitches where an increase or decrease is indicated, and move them in the direction needed to make increases or decreases. For an increase, do not forget to fill the empty needle with the bar from an adjoining stitch.

Sweater Sizes

When these sweaters were designed, I usually had a very specific size in mind—a friend's favorite vest, sleeves long enough for a tall teenage boy, oversize for an adolescent.

Most of the sweaters look well on a wide variety of body shapes, especially considering today's relaxed standards for fit. The individual sweater instructions have overall measurements for the finished sweater, plus a simple schematic drawing with specific shape dimensions. If you have a favorite sweater shape, you can probably adapt most of these designs to fit your requirements. Make a simple drawing of the sweater size

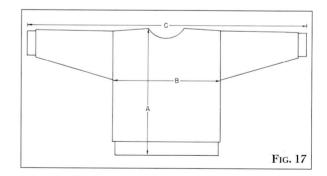

FIG. 17

you want. The most important measurements you will need are: total length of body, width of chest (at underarm), total sleeve length (from cuff across shoulder to other cuff). [See Figure 17.]

Take the total length of body and subtract the border depth (usually 1½ to 2½ inches) to determine the main body length.

Take this figure and multiply by the number of *rows* per inch. This gives you the total number of rows needed to achieve the length you want.

Check this total against the chart. If you need to knit fewer or more rows than appear on the chart, figure out where it best fits the design to delete or add rows. Sometimes it is best to do this at the bottom of the sweater (on the Sea Duck design, for example). Sometimes deletion or addition should occur in the middle of the sweater (as in the Daylily design). Sometimes deletion or addition of rows can occur at the top of the sweater (the Riotous Reindeer design).

Make a photocopy of the chart so you can draw lines or make notes for additions or subtractions for your modified version.

Next take the width of the chest measurement you want and multiply this by the number of *stitches* per inch. Check this total against the chart. If you need to cast on fewer or more stitches than appear on the chart, divide the difference of stitches in half and add or delete equally on both edges of the chart.

Keep in mind that, on drop-shoulder designs, if you add width to the sweater body, you automatically add length to the sleeves. And conversely, if you subtract from body width, you subtract from sleeve length.

Take *your* total desired sleeve length (sleeve plus body width plus sleeve, not including cuffs), and subtract the body width you want from sleeve length. Divide this number by 2 to give the required length of each sleeve. Multiply this figure by the number of *rows* per inch. Check against the sleeve chart, drawing lines for addition or subtraction of rows. Compare your cuff with the decorative cuff. If there is a difference, it is usually easier to add or subtract that difference from the main sleeve rather than altering the decorative cuff border.

When adding extra rows or stitches to charts, you should have no difficulty in extending the designs. Many are repeat designs and are easily extended (Sea Ducks, Victorian Firs, Oak Leaves, Interlocking Fishes, and Oriental Motif). By carefully looking at the irregular designs (Day-lilies, Floral Tapestry, Seashells, Riotous Reindeer, Floral Patchwork, Garden Exotica, and Leaping Cats), you should be able to make logical expansions on the designs. Again, a photocopy of the chart is very helpful for working out your own shape modifications on a particular design.

Washing and Blocking Finished Pieces

It has become a habit with me when either machine or hand knitting to always wash and block my knitted pieces *as I finish them*. This is especially important with machine knitting as the knitting gets very distorted by the weights used in the knitting process. Washing and blocking right away lets you know whether you have truly achieved the shape you were after. With wool, if the shape is slightly off, you can usually block to the desired dimensions. If the piece is really off and cannot be blocked to desired dimensions, you can make necessary adjustments before all the pieces are knit.

Washing wool sweaters is not difficult and does not have to end in disaster if you follow a few basic guidelines. The dreaded result of felted, misshapen wool sweaters is the direct effect of using harsh soaps and too much agitation in the laundering process. Drastic changes in water temperature will also cause felting.

Never put your wool sweater in the washing machine, except for a gentle spin cycle to remove excess rinse water. Never wring out the knitting.

Fill a dish tub or sink with lukewarm water and add a mild detergent or specialty wool soap. Submerge the knitting, gently squeezing to allow water to penetrate fibers. Let it soak for several minutes. Drain the wash water, gently squeezing out excess. Fill the tub or sink again with lukewarm water, gently squeezing the knitting. Drain and repeat the rinsing. On the last rinse, you may add a tablespoon (for a whole sweater) or teaspoon (for a sweater piece) of crème rinse. If you are sensitive to wool, the crème rinse will coat the wool fiber, just as it does your hair, and make it less scratchy.

Wrap and roll the knitting in a towel to remove excess water. Or place it in your washing machine, with a towel to balance the load, and run it through a short final spin cycle.

Lay the damp knitting on a couple of thicknesses of towel. I put the towel and knitting on a fiberglass window screen so air can pass freely above and below. Using a tape measure, spread the knitting gently to your desired dimensions and pin it to the towel.

Let the knitting dry completely before removing the pins.

ABBREVIATIONS USED IN KNITTING INSTRUCTIONS

beg—beginning
cm—centimeter
dec—decrease (ed) (es) (ing)
g—gram
HP—holding position
lb—pound
m—meter

oz—ounce, ounces
rep—repeat(s)
sl—slip
st(s)—stitch(es)
tog—together
WPI—wraps per inch

INTERLOCKING FISHES

The coastal community where we live relies heavily on fishing for year-round employment. We often go to local wharves to buy the freshest fish imaginable for supper. Looking at the fish trays with their numerous varieties is always interesting. Mackerel, hake, cod, haddock, redfish, cusk, monkfish, and the occasional halibut all create a kaleidoscope of shimmering colors.

I started work on the design for this sweater with those fishes in mind. Thinking out the colors coincided with the introduction of Harrisville Designs' new color line. Harrisville dyes the wool before it is spun, allowing them to blend their Shetland Style wools and Tweeds with complex mixes of colors. Their yarns have beautiful depth, reminding me of the way the Impressionists used color.

The original sweater includes four of Harrisville Designs' new colors and two of their old colors. I have included what I hope are reasonable substitutes for the old colors. Of course you should feel free to make entirely different color choices. Harrisville's Monet Blue, Purple, and Lagoon Blue could set up a wonderful, deep sea mood. Or you could go tropical with their 2-ply worsteds in American Beauty, Butterscotch, and Magenta, to get you started.

This sweater fits a variety of body shapes from size 8 to size 12. It was sized to fit a growing young woman who likes her sweaters to sit at the waist. If you are long-waisted, you may want to add to the length. I suggest doing this at the bottom of the sweater so you do not have to alter the shawl collar.

I have included instructions for both hand and machine knitters up to the cuff bands, lower border, and collar. The collar would be impossible to knit on a machine without creating a center-back seam, which did not seem desirable. So I suggest that machine knitters knit the borders and collar by hand. (The collar chart is divided at the center only because it does not fit on one page. The collar should be knit in one continuous piece.)

This sweater could also be knit with a simple collar band, such as the ones on the Oak Leaves or Leaping Cats vests. Just pick up the number of stitches indicated for plackets plus collar, and work a simple border with contrast-color edging and lining.

GAUGE

- 18 sts and 24 rows = 4 inches (4½ sts and 6 rows = 1 inch)
- Borders: 4¾ sts and 6 rows = 1 inch

Note: This is the hand-knit gauge. Machine knitters may have to knit more rows to achieve the desired total length. These rows should be added at the bottom of the sweater body, as indicated on the chart.

EQUIPMENT

- Size 7 or 8, 24-inch circular needle for body of sweater
- Size 5 or 6, 24-inch circular needle for borders and collar
- Optional: Size 5 or 6 double-pointed needles for seamless cuffs

(Adjust needle sizes as needed to achieve correct gauge.)

- Machine: Large-gauge machine set up for intarsia knitting

  Tension setting: 7–8 for body of sweater

SUGGESTED YARNS AND NOTIONS

- 6 buttons (½-inch)
- Harrisville Designs' 2-ply Tweeds or 2-ply worsteds.

- 6 skeins total, each skein 3.5 ozs, approximately 200 yds (900 yds/lb, 13 WPI)
- 1 each of the following:

  Dawn Mist (D)

  True Blue (B)

  Clover (lavender) (L)

  Turquoise (T)

  Mulberry (M)

  Aster (A)

Equivalent yarn: Any yarn with approximately 900 yds per pound or that knits up as a general worsted weight in the above gauge. (Please read "Choosing Your Yarns," pages 13–15, if you plan to substitute yarns.)

OVERALL MEASUREMENTS

- Total chest : 44 inches
- Total sleeve: 18½ inches (includes 2¼-inch cuff)
- Body length at shoulder: 21¼ inches (includes 2¼-inch border)

INSTRUCTIONS

Back: With needles/machine tension for body of sweater, cast on 92 sts with waste yarn and pull cord method (page 18).

- Begin chart at lower right-hand corner, attach-

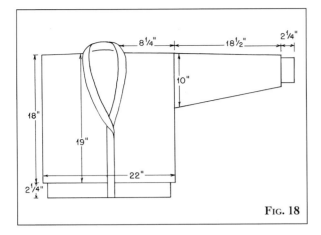

FIG. 18

ing yarns as indicated. Weave in tails as you knit (pages 23–25).

◻ Proceed up chart, attaching yarn marker for sleeve where indicated.
◻ Shape shoulders with short rows (pages 20–23).
◻ Knit off shoulder and back-neck sts using pull cord/waste yarn (page 18).

Fronts: It is helpful to knit both fronts at the same time to keep length and shaping uniform.

◻ Cast on 46 sts for each front, using waste yarn/pull cord.
◻ Proceed up chart, beginning neck shaping as shown and attaching yarn markers where indicated for sleeves.
◻ Shape shoulders with short rows.
◻ Knit off using pull cord/waste yarn.

◻ Block sweater pieces (pages 27–28) and assemble shoulders of front and backs using invisible grafting technique (page 19).

Sleeves: Cast on 52 sts with waste yarn/pull cord.

◻ Start chart from the lower right, attaching yarns and weaving in tails as you knit.
◻ Proceed up chart for 5 rows. Increase 1 st at beginning and end of row, using full-fashion increases (page 26).
◻ Continue increases every 5 rows, following the chart, until you have 92 sts.
◻ Cast off with regular cast-off where indicated on chart. (This is near the top of a fish tail row. You can keep it simple and cast off following the previous row's colors.)

Cuff Borders: For a *seamless* cuff border, sew sleeve to body between yarn markers, then sew underarm and side seams. Work seamless cuff border on double-pointed needles. (Cuff border may also be knit flat before sleeves are attached, using the needles indicated for borders.)

◻ Pick up the lower-sleeve sts and remove waste yarn/pull cord (page 18).
◻ Attach color M and knit 1, knit 2 together across row. Cuff is knit on 36 sts.
◻ Follow chart for cuff border.
◻ Last row of chart is cast-off row. Cast off using regular cast-off method.

Lower Border: After side seams are sewn, work the lower border.

◻ With needles indicated for borders, pick up sts around bottom of body.
◻ Remove pull cord/waste yarn.
◻ Attach color M and knit 1 row, decreasing 8 sts evenly spaced. Border is worked on 176 sts.
◻ Follow chart for lower border.
◻ Last row of chart is cast-off row. Cast off using regular cast-off method.
◻ Slip stitch rolled edge to inside of border.

Right Front Buttonhole Placket: With needles indicated for border and color M, pick up 50 sts along placket edge, beginning at first dec of neck opening. Row 1 is worked from lower edge of decorative border up to neck opening.

◻ Row 1: Purl
◻ Row 2: Attach color A and purl to within last 2 sts. Attach color M and knit these 2 sts.

Interlocking Fishes

Front, Back, and Sleeve

sleeve edge

sleeve edge

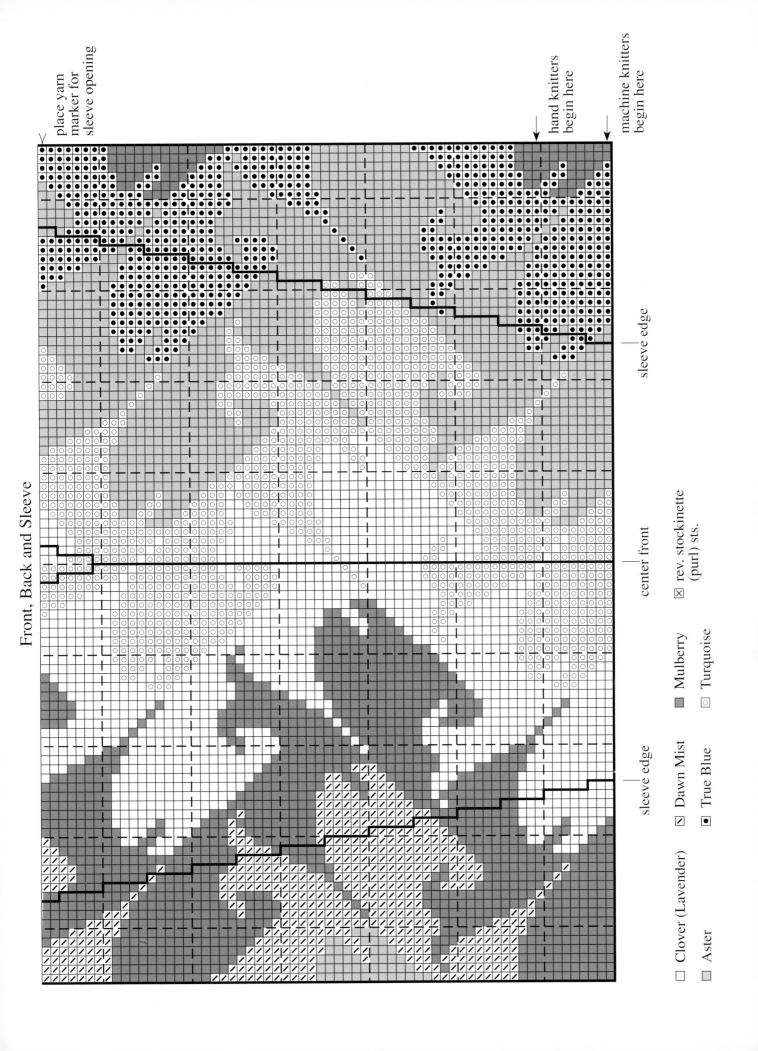

Front, Back and Sleeve

place yarn marker for sleeve opening

hand knitters begin here

machine knitters begin here

sleeve edge

center front

sleeve edge

□ Clover (Lavender)   ⊠ Dawn Mist   ■ Mulberry   ⊠ rev. stockinette (purl) sts.

▨ Aster   • True Blue   ○ Turquoise

Collar: Work on 140 sts. with no center seam.

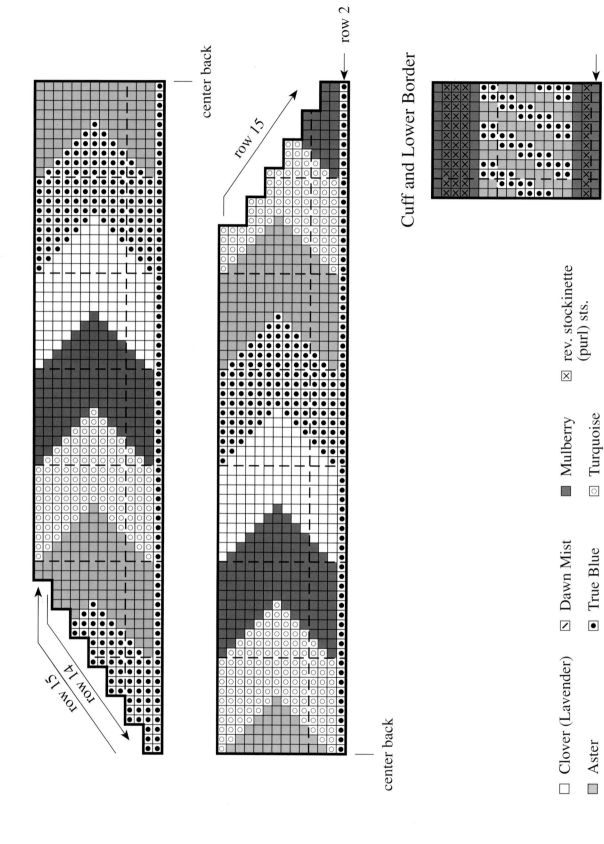

Cuff and Lower Border

□ Clover (Lavender) ☒ Dawn Mist ■ Mulberry ☒ rev. stockinette (purl) sts.

▨ Aster ● True Blue ⊡ Turquoise

▫ Row 7: Purl
▫ Row 8: Purl
▫ Rows 9 & 10: Repeat buttonhole rows 3 and 4.
▫ Row 11: Knit
▫ Row 12: Cast off.
▫ Slip stitch cast-off row to first row of band.

Left Front Button Placket: Starting at bottom edge of decorative border, pick up 50 sts with color M. Row 1 is worked from first decrease of neck opening *down* to edge of border.
▫ Row 1: Purl
▫ Row 2: Knit 2 sts M, attach color A and purl remaining sts.
▫ Row 3: Knit 48 A sts, purl 2 M sts.
▫ Row 4: Knit 2 M sts, purl 48 A sts.
▫ Row 5: Attach color T and knit across row, including 2 M edge sts.
▫ Create purl edge by knitting row 6 and purling row 7.
▫ Rows 8–11: Stockinette stitch (knit odd rows, purl even rows).
▫ Row 12: Cast off.
▫ Slip stitch cast-off row to first row of placket.

Collar: With needles indicated for collar and color B, pick up 144 sts around neck edge from buttonhole placket to button placket. Remove waste yarn/pull cord.
▫ With right side of sweater facing you, knit first row, decreasing 4 sts across back of neck. Collar is worked on 140 sts.

▫ Row 2: Begin collar chart here. This designates right side of collar. Knit this row.
▫ Row 3: Purl
▫ Row 4: Shaping of shawl collar begins on this row. Knit, following chart to last 3 sts. Turn for short row (see pages 20–23).
▫ Continue following chart to Row 14, shaping collar at both edges with short rows.
▫ At Row 14, continue across to *end* of collar, including all short-row sts, maintaining established chevron pattern. (Note arrow on chart.)
▫ At Row 15, work last row of chart, working to other end of collar, including all short row sts. Maintain established chevron pattern.
▫ Attach color B and work 2 more rows in stockinette stitch.
▫ Work 3 rows of reverse stockinette stitch to make purl edge for fold on collar.
▫ ***Collar Lining:*** Attach color L and work 2 rows of stockinette stitch.
▫ Shape collar lining with short rows, leaving 3 sts at each edge unworked, 5 times.
▫ When lining shaping is complete, work 2 rows to include all short row sts.
▫ Fold collar at purl edge. Secure last row of lining sts to first row of collar with tapestry needle (page 20).

Finishing: Check to make sure all yarn tails are secured. Trim to 1 inch.
▫ Gently wash and block sweater.
▫ Attach buttons opposite buttonholes.

SEASHELLS

The Seashells design was created for my mother, a thank-you for her patience and support over the years. One of my earliest memories is sitting on the floor making designs with boxes of buttons while my mother sewed for my sisters and me. She played a big role in shaping my hands-on approach to life. She still fills her days with gardening, cooking, baking, and sewing.

Diverse influences merged to shape the Seashells sweater. There are beautiful sand beaches in Phippsburg, Maine, which we walk several times a week. The shells, ocean debris, and sand patterns change constantly. The weathered shells are my favorites—moon shells bleached to soft shades of blue, lavender, and gray, mussel shells worn down to reveal mother-of-pearl, and starfish and whelks in endless variations.

A book in our local library, *Patterns from Paradise, The Art of Tahitian Quilting*, by Vicki Roggioli, is filled with some of the most vibrant, wonderful quilt designs imaginable. The quilters use a fold-and-cut technique to create symmetrical and complex patterns. The designs reflect their rich island environment, from tropical flowers to seashells. These designs are worked out on large bedsheets, folded into fourths. It is similar to cutting a snowflake from folded paper. The design mirrors itself in four repeats.

The batwing shape of this sweater lends itself beautifully to a four-section repeat. When knitting up the design, knit the two front charts first. Then photocopy the charts, trim one down the center front, and tape them together, matching up rows and lower edge. Now you are ready to proceed down the back. It is fun to knit the bodies and sleeves all in one; don't be afraid to try it.

Using pale yellows in the background sets up a few color restrictions. Pinks have a tendency to look very sickly next to yellow, like gooey Easter candies. Beiges can look dirty. However, corals and apricot/orange, smoky blues, lavender blues, deep iris, navy, sea greens, soft jades, and teals all hold their character well next to yellow.

You could also easily translate this into a two-color design. That is how most of the Tahitian appliquéd quilts are worked.

The borders are worked in reverse stockinette stitch and garter stitch. The use of a textured border carries through the theme of sand patterns used in the background. I did try various decorative Fair Isle-type borders, but as my husband pointed out, they were "gilding the lily," and I finally settled on the two-color border shown here.

The gauge is large: 3¼ stitches and 5¼ rows per inch. Most of the variegated background was knit with blends of 3 strands; 2 Jagger Spun 2/8s with various pearl silks, angora/silk blends, mohair, or thin cotton bouclés. The shell motifs are also done in many triple blends, utilizing the same yarns as above plus Harrisville Designs' Shetland Style wools and Tweeds. Pearl silks and cottons give a wonderful subtle sheen to the shells. The seaweed motifs are a double blend using a novelty rainbow-dyed yarn of rayon and silk. The colors in this yarn include maroons, purples, bittersweet, and turquoise. I blended it with sport weight yarns in blues, teals, and sea greens.

This is a "one size fits all" pattern. To lengthen the design, add rows at the bottom either on the body or the border—or both.

It is one of the few patterns where I have not included machine knitting instructions. To knit it by machine, you would have to make it in two sections with a seam down the middle back, which I felt was not desirable.

GAUGE
- Body: 15 sts and 21 rows = 4 inches (3¼ sts and 5¼ rows = 1 inch)
- Borders: 4 sts and 7 rows = 1 inch in garter stitch

SUGGESTED NEEDLES
- Size 8 or 9, 24-inch circular needle for main body and borders
- Optional: Size 8 or 9 double-pointed needles for seamless cuffs
- Size 5, 24-inch circular needle for borders and rolled cuff edge
- Optional: Size 5 double-pointed needles for seamless rolled cuff edge

(Adjust needle sizes as needed to achieve correct gauge.)

SUGGESTED YARNS AND NOTIONS
- Five ⅝-inch buttons
- Multiple yarns combined to knit up equivalent to bulky weight, with approximately 700 yds per lb (9 WPI). The WPI is more important on multiple yarn combinations than yards per pound (see page 14).
- 1 lb 8 oz for background (yellows)

□ 3½ to 4 oz corals/apricots for starfish and whelk shells

□ For mussel shells, moon shells, and borders:
3 oz pale blues, grays, lavenders
3 oz medium blues, grays, and lavenders
3 oz dark blues and purples

The yarn combinations include Jagger Spun Maine Line wool 2/8s; Halcyon Yarn's Victorian 2-ply wool, 5/2 pearl cottons, 2/12 and 2/8 pearl silks, mohair, Scottish tapestry wool, Lollipop (mercerized cotton/rayon slub), and flake cotton; Harrisville Designs' sport weight Shetland Style, worsted weight and single-ply Tweeds; Reynolds Kitten (acrylic/wool blend); novelty blends of silk/rayon, alpaca/silk, and cotton/wool. "Choosing Your Yarns," pages 13–15, explains in detail about combining or substituting yarns. A detailed list of the yarns I used for Seashells can be found on pages 115–116.

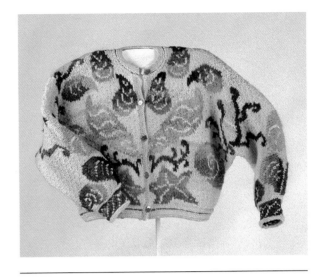

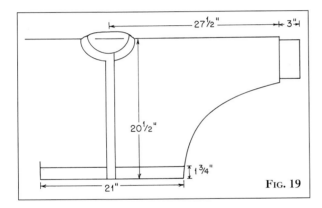

FIG. 19

OVERALL MEASUREMENTS

□ Length from shoulder: 20½ inches (includes 1¾-inch border)
□ Sleeve length from center back to cuff: 30½ inches (includes 3-inch border cuff)
□ Total width at waist: 42 inches

INSTRUCTIONS

Fronts: You may wish to knit fronts at the same time. I knit them separately so I could work out the colors and not have to unravel so much if I did not like a particular color combination. If you knit the fronts separately, the first one can be cast off onto pull cord/waste yarn or put onto another circular needle. Add rubber needle guards to prevent the knitting from slipping off.

□ With larger needles, cast on 42 sts with waste yarn/pull cord method (pages 17–18). It is also possible to use a simple cast-on (pages 18–19), but I recommend the other method.

□ Follow chart, beginning at lower right corner, increasing and casting on sts as you work up chart for sleeve shaping.

□ For neck shaping, work short rows (pages 20–23) where multiple decreases appear on chart. Use full-fashion decreases (page 26) for single-stitch decreases.

Back: When fronts are complete, photocopy both charts. Trim one down the middle and tape them together, matching up grid lines and lower edges. Turn charts 180°; the back is knit from the shoulders down.

□ Start chart where arrow indicates at shoulder of right front, knitting across to neck edge.

□ Cast on 22 sts, following colors on chart. Attach left front (pick up sts and remove pull cord/waste yarn, if used [see page 18]), and continue across chart to edge.

□ Follow charts, casting off sts and then decreasing as you shape the underarm/side curve.

□ When back is complete, keep lower back sts on needles.

□ (Note: After center shell motif is knit, you can actually knit the rest of the sweater using one chart. Simply follow each row of chart across to the center, then reverse direction and follow the same row back across for second half of back.)

Sew side and underarm seams. Note: If you are using double-pointed needles for seamless cuffs,

Seashells

Right Front and Back

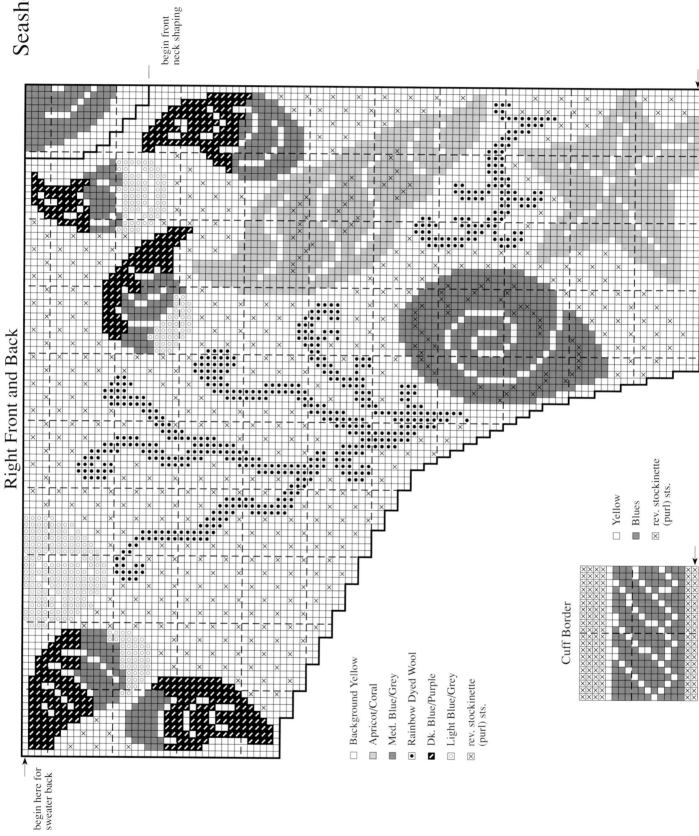

begin here for
sweater back

Legend:
- ☐ Background Yellow
- ☐ Apricot/Coral
- ▨ Med. Blue/Grey
- ⊡ Rainbow Dyed Wool
- ◪ Dk. Blue/Purple
- ⊙ Light Blue/Grey
- ☒ rev. stockinette (purl) sts.

Cuff Border

Legend:
- ☐ Yellow
- ▨ Blues
- ☒ rev. stockinette (purl) sts.

Seashells

Left Front and Back

Legend:
- ☐ Background Yellow
- ▨ Apricot/Coral
- ▨ Med. Blue/Grey
- ▨ Rainbow Dyed Wool
- ◪ Dk. Blue/Purple
- ◉ Light Blue/Grey
- ☒ rev. stockinette (purl) sts.

begin sweater front

begin front neck shaping

sew seam all the way to sleeve edge. If you are using a circular needle for the cuffs, sew to within a few inches of sleeve edge to allow end of sleeve to open out flat.

Lower Border: the lower back sts are still on needle. Pick up lower left and right front sts onto same needles and remove pull cord/waste yarn.
- Change to smaller needles and, with right sides facing, knit 1 row in background color.
- Work two rows of reverse stockinette stitch (knit 1 row, purl 1 row)
- Knit 4th row.
- Change to contrast color (blue) and purl 1 row.
- Change to background color and knit 1 row.
- Continue to knit next 6 rows (garter stitch).
- Cast off.

Cuff Borders: With larger needles and background color, pick up 1 st between every other row bar on sleeve edge, for a total of 38 sts.
- Follow chart for cuff, knitting 2 rows of reverse stockinette stitch.
- On first plain row of chart (in contrast color — blues), before pattern begins, dec 4 sts evenly spaced across row. Continue to follow chart on 34 sts.
- Change to smaller needles to knit rolled cuff.
- Rolled cuff: Knit 4 rows in reverse stockinette stitch. Fourth row is cast-off row.
- If cuff was knit flat, finish sewing underarm seam and cuff.

Right Front Buttonhole Placket: With smaller needle and background color, pick up 76 sts on right front center edge.
- With right side facing, purl 1 row.
- Knit 1 row

- Buttonhole row: Knit 12 sts, cast off 2 sts, (knit 18 sts, cast off 2 sts) 3 times, knit to end of row.
- Next row: Knit to cast-off sts, (cast on 2 sts, knit 18 sts) 3 times, cast on 2 sts, knit to end of row.
- Knit 1 row.
- Knit cast-off row.

Left Front Button Placket: With smaller needles and background color, pick up 76 sts on left front opening.
- With right side facing, purl 1 row.
- Knit 1 row.
- Knit 3 more rows (garter stitch).
- Cast-off in knit stitch.

Neck Edge: With smaller circular needle and background color, pick up 64 sts around neck edge, including front plackets.
- Begin work with right side facing. Purl 1 row.
- Knit 1 row.
- Attach contrast color (blues), but do not break off background color, and knit 1 row.
- Turn sweater so right side is facing you, pick up background color, and knit 1 row.
- Continue with background color in garter stitch, making a buttonhole on this row by knitting to within 5 sts of right side edge, casting off 2 sts and knitting last 3 sts.
- On next row, knit 3 sts, cast on 2 sts over buttonhole, continue to knit to end of row.
- Knit 2 more rows in garter stitch.
- Cast off.

Finishing:
- Sew buttons on left side to match buttonholes.
- Gently wash and block sweater (pages 27–28).

SEA DUCKS

T he numbers of sea ducks—common ei-
ders, surf scoters—and loons on the north
end of Casco Bay have been growing over
the past few years. It seems like an odd reversal
in these times of endangered wildlife. We watch
them all year long: their late winter courting
rituals, the lone elegant males during nesting

season, and the wonderful rafts of mothers, year-
lings, and ducklings in the summer and fall
months.

A modern Peruvian rug in a home furnishing
store provided the actual elements for the design
of this sweater. When I saw the rug, I wondered
if the Peruvian weaver had been influenced by

M.C. Escher, or if Escher had been influenced by the ancient weaving designs of Peru. Who knows! They both influenced me, along with the local sea ducks.

This is a large man's sweater, a bold design originally created for a six-foot-three, long-armed teenager. It also fits comfortably on six-foot variety males. If you want to shorten the body length, do so at the bottom of the design so the central duck's head does not get lopped off by the sweater neck. The sleeves can be shortened at top or bottom or both.

Bright foggy mornings and the iridescent nature of duck feathers guided my yarn combinations for the light/dark colorway. For the light ducks, I used heathery, pale Shetland Style with flecks of blue, gray, or pale lilac in combination with natural off-whites, pearl grays, and creamy whites. Mohair, slubby cottons, and silk/angora blends add textural interest.

The dark ducks blend deep-colored Harrisville Designs' Shetland Style wools in greens, blues, and purples with navy, teal, and deep greens in both sport weight yarn and mohair. Heavy tweeds were used singly. Thin homespun–type tweed wools and cotton/wool novelty blends add textural variety. You could also include pearl cottons or silks to add luster to the dark ducks.

The multicolor duck sweater was a good excuse to try out some beautiful Tipperary Tweeds (alas, as we go to press—we learn Tipperary Tweeds are no longer available), filling in with what I had on hand. If you have a good collection of wools, just map out the five major color bands you want to use, then have fun making your own custom blends.

You will notice that the sweaters in the photograph are mirror images. This is because the multicolor version was knit by machine, which yields a knitted piece that is the reverse of the image on the chart.

GAUGE

- Body: Hand knitting—15 sts and 22 rows = 4 inches (3¾ sts and 5½ rows = 1 inch); machine knitting—15 sts and 23 rows = 4 inches (3¾ sts and 5¾ rows = 1 inch)
- Borders: 4 sts and 6 rows = 1 inch

EQUIPMENT

- Size 8 or 9, 24-inch circular needle for body of sweater
- Size 6 or 7, 24-inch circular needle for borders
- Optional: Size 6 or 7 double-pointed needles for seamless cuffs and neck borders

(Adjust needle sizes as needed to achieve correct gauge.)

- *Machine:* large-gauge machine set up for intarsia knitting
  Tension setting 8.5–9 for body of sweater
  Tension setting 7.5 for cuffs and borders
  Tension setting 6 for linings

SUGGESTED YARNS

- Bulky yarns plus combinations of lighter-weight yarns to match bulky weight (approximately 600 to 900 yds/lb, 10 WPI).
- Total weight 2.11 to 2.17 lbs (The multicolor ducks sweater weighs more because the Tipperary Tweeds are dense yarns and weigh more per yard than the blends of lighter yarns.)
- For dark/light ducks:

Light combination: 1 lb mixed yarns

Dark combination: 1.25 lbs mixed yarns

Approximately 2 ozs red combination for border stripe

Linings: Use dark combinations

▢ For multicolor ducks:

8 oz each of 5 colorways—blues, rusty reds, charcoal/blacks, grays, and dark greens.

"Choosing Your Yarns," pages 13–15, explains in detail about combining or substituting yarns. Detailed lists of yarns used in both sweaters are found on pages 116–117.

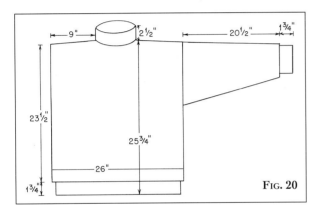

FIG. 20

OVERALL MEASUREMENTS

▢ Length of body: 25¾ inches (includes 1¾-inch border for dark/light ducks, 2-inch border for multicolor ducks)

▢ Total chest: 52 inches

▢ Sleeve: 22¼ inches (includes 1¾-inch cuff for dark/light ducks, 3-inch cuff for multicolor ducks)

INSTRUCTIONS

Note: The multicolor ducks sweater was knit by machine, the dark/light ducks version by hand. Since the machine tension differs from the hand-knit in rows per inch, machine knitters should work additional rows at bottom of chart, as shown.

Back or Front: With larger circular needle, or machine tension 8.5 to 9, cast on 96 sts, using simple or invisible cast-on for hand knitters (pages 18–19), and waste yarn/pull cord method for machine knitters (page 18).

▢ Start chart at lower right-hand corner, attaching colors as indicated and securing tails as you knit (pages 23–25).

▢ Follow up the chart. Mark for sleeve opening with a yarn marker where indicated on chart.

▢ Use short rows to shape neck and shoulders (pages 20–23).

▢ Cast off neck sts with pull cord and waste yarn (page 18). Optional: Put neck sts on holder.

▢ If hand knitting, cast off shoulders using regular cast-off method. This is a heavy sweater and benefits from being secured at the shoulders with a seam.

▢ Machine knitters may cast off with pull cord/waste yarn. When back and front are complete,

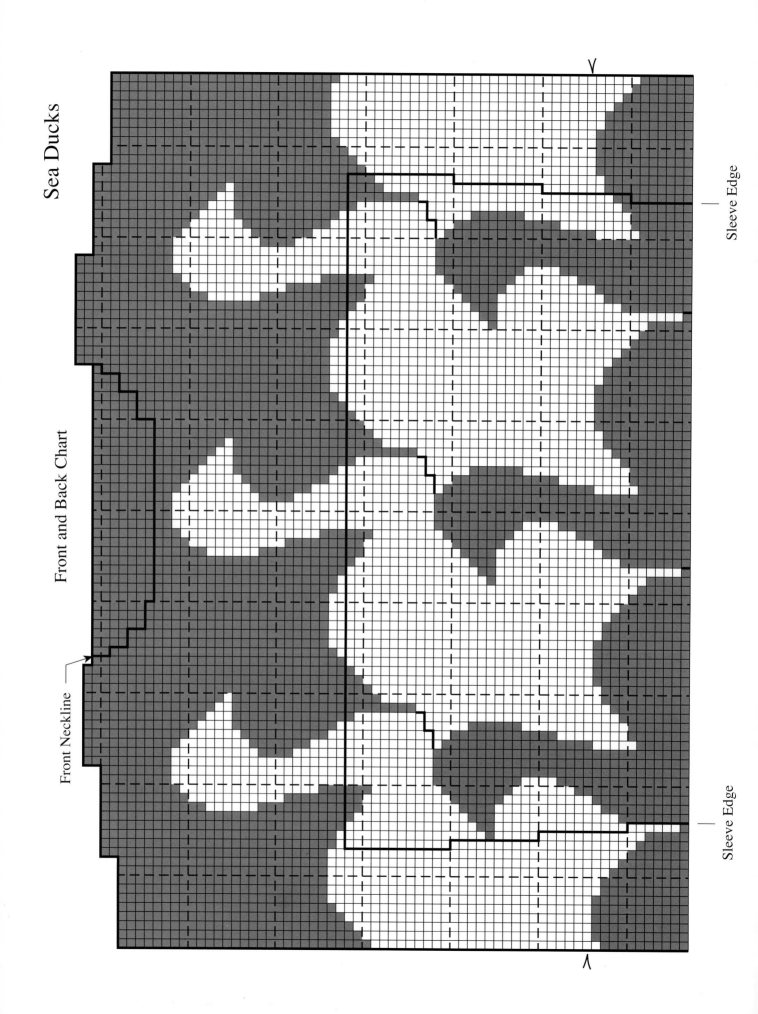

Sea Ducks

Front and Back Chart

Front Neckline

Sleeve Edge

Sleeve Edge

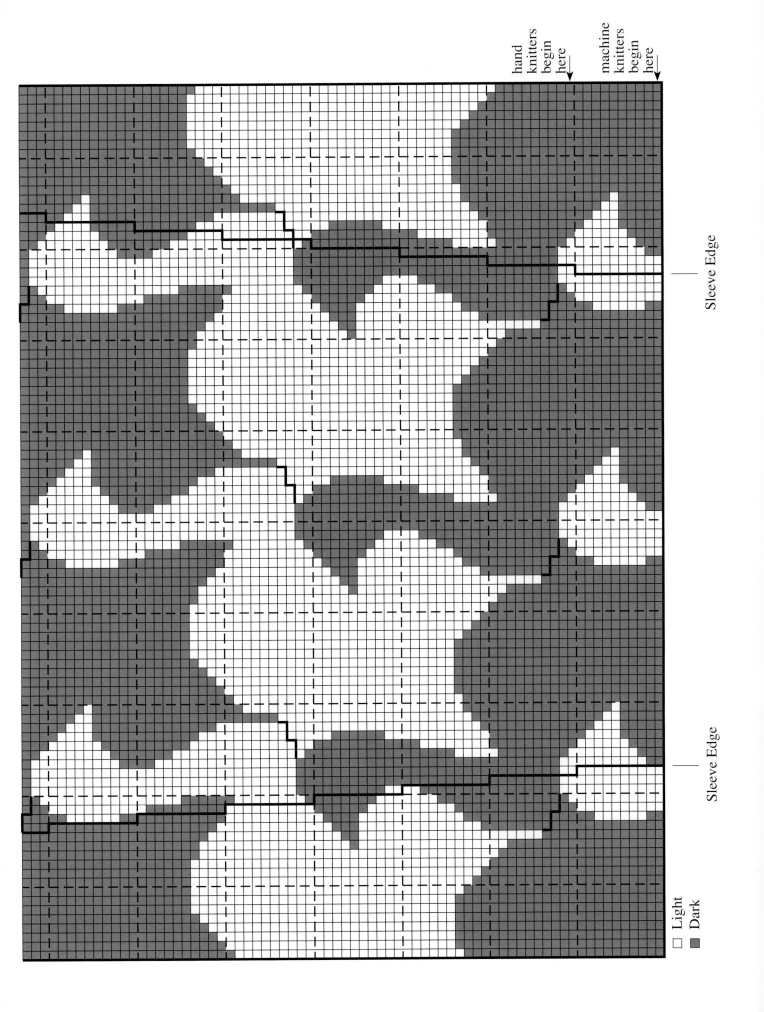

hand knitters begin here

machine knitters begin here

Sleeve Edge

Sleeve Edge

☐ Light
▨ Dark

Sea Ducks

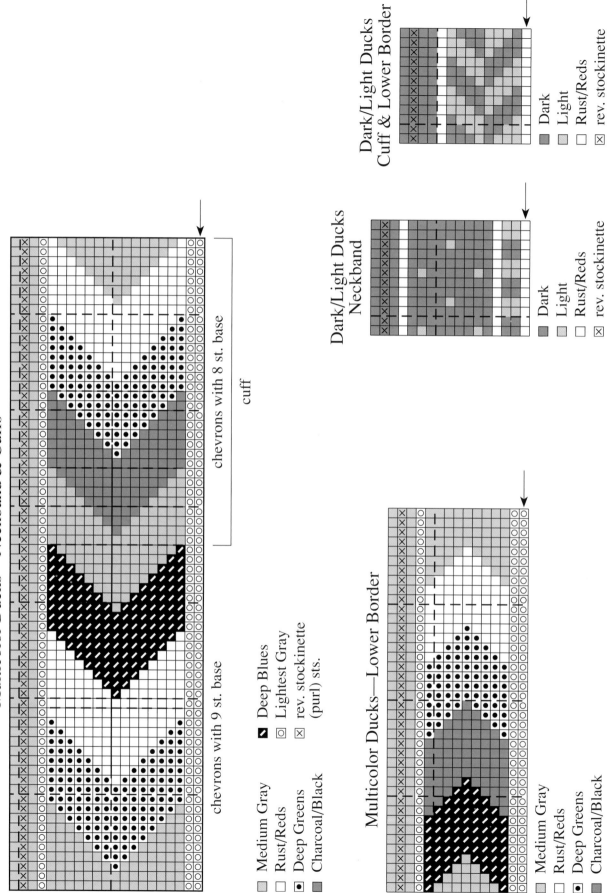

Multicolor Ducks—Neckband & Cuffs

chevrons with 9 st. base

chevrons with 8 st. base

cuff

☐ Medium Gray	■ Deep Blues	
☐ Rust/Reds	◉ Lightest Gray	
● Deep Greens	☒ rev. stockinette	
▨ Charcoal/Black	(purl) sts.	

Dark/Light Ducks Cuff & Lower Border

☐ Dark	
■ Light	
☐ Rust/Reds	
☒ rev. stockinette (purl) sts.	

Dark/Light Ducks Neckband

☐ Dark	
☐ Light	
☐ Rust/Reds	
☒ rev. stockinette (purl) sts.	

Multicolor Ducks—Lower Border

☐ Medium Gray	▨ Deep Blues	
☐ Rust/Reds	◉ Lightest Gray	
● Deep Greens	☒ rev. stockinette	
■ Charcoal/Black	(purl) sts.	

rehang shoulders, right sides together. Set tension 2 settings higher, knit 1 row, and cast off with tapestry needle.

- Check over all yarn tails to make sure they are secure. Trim tails to 1 inch. Gently wash and block sweater pieces (pages 27–28) as you complete them (particularly if machine knit).

Sleeves: With larger circular needle, or main tension setting on machine, cast on 58 sts using waste yarn/pull cord method.

- Follow chart, increasing 1 st at each edge every 10 rows, until you have a total of 76 sts. Use full-fashion increases (page 26).
- When top of chart is reached, cast off with regular cast-off method.

Neckband: Sew front and back together at right shoulder. Machine knitters use method described above.

- Option: For seamless neckband, sew *both* shoulders together and use double-pointed needles to work neckband.
- Using smaller circular needle, or machine tension 7.5, pick up 70 sts around neck — 68 sts on waste yarn (or holders) plus 1 edge st at each shoulder.
- Work on 70 sts for dark/light duck neckband. For multicolor ducks neckband, decrease 2 sts on neck to work 68 sts.
- Choose approximately 3 yds for each chevron on the multicolor ducks neckband (the same applies for the cuffs). If neckband/cuffs are not knit in the round on double-pointed needles, match up colors at beginning and ending of second row so chevrons are continuous when ends of bands are sewn together. Note that 4 of the chevrons are 8 sts wide, 4 are 9 sts wide.
- *Machine knitters:* Use garter bar to reverse knitting for reverse stockinette stitch row as indicated on chart. (See pages 19–20 for tips on knitting this row.)
- When chart is complete, attach yarn for lining (use a lightweight combination), and knit lining to same depth as outside of neck border. Use one size smaller needles, and lower tension on machine border linings.
- *Hand knitters:* Use a tapestry needle to secure stitches of last row of lining to first row of border (see page 20).

- *Machine knitters:* Bring up first row of neckband and hang on needles. Change tension dial 2 settings higher and knit 1 row. Cast off, using a tapestry needle.
- Sew remaining shoulders together. Sew collar and collar lining.

Cuff Borders:

- Note: If using double-pointed needles to knit seamless cuff bands, attach sleeves to body and sew underarm and side seams before working cuffs.
- Pick up sts of sleeve on smaller needles, remove waste yarn (page 18).
- *Hand knitters:* Attach yarn for contrast stripe and work first row of chart, decreasing as follows: Knit first 3 sts, knit 2 tog across, knit last 3 sts singly. Cuffs are worked on 32 sts.
- *Machine knitters:* Rehang sts of sleeve as follows: first and last 3 sts singly, all the rest double for a total of 32 needles.
- Follow appropriate chart for cuff. For multicolor version, be careful to match up chevron colors, as noted above under "Neckband."
- *Machine knitters:* Use garter bar to reverse knitting for reverse stockinette stitch row.
- When chart is complete, attach lining yarn and knit to same depth as border, using same method as for neckband. Secure edge with same method as for neckband.

Lower Border: Work lower border by hand if you want seamless borders. If you work them by machine, do so *before* assembling side seams. The following instructions assume you are making a seamless lower border.

- After sleeves are attached and underarm and side seams are sewn, pick up all the sts around lower edge of front and back, with smaller circular needle. Remove waste yarn/pull cord if you used them.
- Follow appropriate chart for lower band. For multicolor version, follow instructions under "Neckband" above, but use 2-yard lengths for each color, and continue around bottom of sweater in established chevron pattern.
- Use same methods for working lining and securing edge as used on cuffs and necks.

Wash and block sweater, if you did not already wash individual pieces.

GARDEN EXOTICA

I love bright colors in winter. I grew up in Southern California with bougainvilleas sprawled across fences and roofs, poinsettias as tall as houses, and botanical gardens that sported year-round displays of exotic-leaved plants. It was those plants with brilliantly colored leaves, the ones where you are hard-pressed to define where the leaves end and the flowers begin, that inspired the Garden Exotica design.

The friend for whom it was knit shares my sense of adventure in design and color. I was free to explore ideas of asymmetrical design, plus use all my favorite colors, and know my friend would be pleased.

For her I created a snug little vest that fits a surprising variety of body shapes. If you are tall or long-waisted, you might want to add five to ten rows on the lower edge. It was sized to sit at the waist.

This vest is really fun to knit. Each piece is totally different, so there is no chance of getting bored with repeating motifs. It knits up very fast and would be a good project for those of you who are experimenting with blending yarns for the first time. Most of the blended yarns are made up of two sport weight yarns. I also used small amounts of rainbow-dyed loopy mohair and other textured novelty yarns that knit up as worsted weight when used singly.

The tweed in the background is my all-time favorite. It is the blue of iris, periwinkles, or campanulas, with just a hint of violet. The reds, apricots, and sea greens are blends of many yarns. If blending yarns does not appeal to you, look for yarns in the basic color groups to substitute.

GAUGE

- Body: 16 stitches and 24 rows = 4 inches (4 sts and 6 rows = 1 inch)
- Borders: 4¼ sts and 7 rows = 1 inch

Note: This is the hand-knit gauge. Machine knitters may need to knit a few more rows to achieve desired finished length. Add them at the bottom of the charts, as shown on the charts. Remember also to add more stitches as required when picking up along the front edges to knit the front and neck borders.

EQUIPMENT

- Size 7 or 8, 24-inch circular needle for body
- Size 5, 24-inch circular needle for border

(Adjust needle sizes as needed to achieve correct gauge.)

- Size F crochet hook for armhole edge and button loops
- Machine: large-gauge machine set up for intarsia knitting
  Tension setting 7–8 for body
  Tension setting 5.5–6 for borders

SUGGESTED YARNS AND NOTIONS

- 4 buttons (⅝-inch)
- Custom blends of yarns, thin yarns doubled, or average worsted weights used singly (700 to 800 yds/lb, 10 WPI).
- Total weight of sweater: 11.2 oz.
- Allow approximately 8 oz of yarn for background: 1 cone of Harrisville Designs' worsted weight tweed, True Blue.
- Allow approximately 6 oz, divided into 3 color groups, for florals and vines: 2 oz reds/pinks, 2 oz apricots/corals, 2 oz sea greens.
- Border linings and rolled neck edge were knit in background color and are included in above yarn requirement.

Yarns combined in this sweater were: Harrisville Designs' worsted weight and sport weight Tweeds and sport weight Shetland Style; Halcyon Yarn's sport weight Victorian 2-ply, mohairs, 10/2 pearl cottons and 2/12 pearl silks; and Jagger Spun Maine Line 2/20 wools. Novelty yarns included: space-dyed loopy mohair, nubbly rayon/acrylic/cotton mix, rayon silk twist, and alpaca sport weight. A detailed list of yarns and colors used appears on page 117. "Choosing Your Yarns," pages 13–15, explains in detail about combining or substituting yarns.

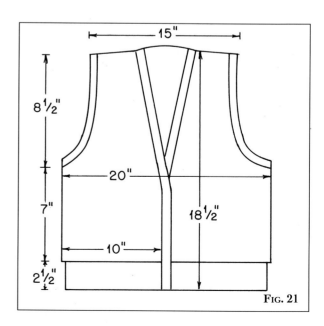

FIG. 21

Dear Knitters,

Even in these days of computer-assisted layout, errors occasionally creep in. We regret the inconvenience this causes. Please note the following errata in two of the designs in *Masterpiece Sweaters*.

LEAPING CATS—CHART, page 62

See below for placement of eyes, whiskers, and spots on two of the cats

INTERLOCKING FISHES—DIRECTIONS, page 32

The instructions for Rows 3 through 6 of the buttonhole band were accidentally cut from the top of the page. Page 32 should begin thus:

- □ Row 3: Purl 2 M sts, change to color A and knit 3 sts, cast off 2 sts (for buttonhole). [Knit 7 sts, cast off 2 sts] 5 times. Knit last 2 sts.
- □ Row 4: Purl, casting on 2 sts at each buttonhole. Knit last 2 M sts.
- □ Row 5: Purl 2 M sts, attach color T and knit.
- □ Row 6: Knit

Then work Rows 7 through 12 as described in your book.

...o shape shoulders and back

...s and neck sts on holders or
...cord/waste yarn.

...houlders (see page 19). Sew

...k to double crochet 2 rows
...in background color.
...row in contrast color.

...sing smaller circular needle,
...und bottom edge.
...kground color, decreasing 26
...ront, 13 sts on back, 6 sts on

...8 sts, following lower border

...der chart is complete, attach
...or and knit 14 more rows (or
...ne depth as border).

...tapestry needle to secure last
...first row of border (page 20).

...strongly recommend knitting the border by hand to avoid interrupting the pattern at side seams. If you opt for knitting the border by machine, it will have to be knit in sections. Rehang left front, decreasing 6 sts. Rehang right front, decreasing 6 sts. Rehang back decreasing 14 sts. Follow lower border

---

□ Put shoulder sts on holder or knit off onto waste yarn/pull cord (page 18).

Back: Cast on 84 sts using same method as used for fronts.

□ Follow chart, decreasing for armholes as indicated on chart.

Garden Exotica

Front and
Neck Borders

Periwinkle Blue/Purple Tweed

Apricot/Coral

Reds/Pinks

Teal/Sea Green

rev. stockinette
(purl) sts.

rolled
edge

Front

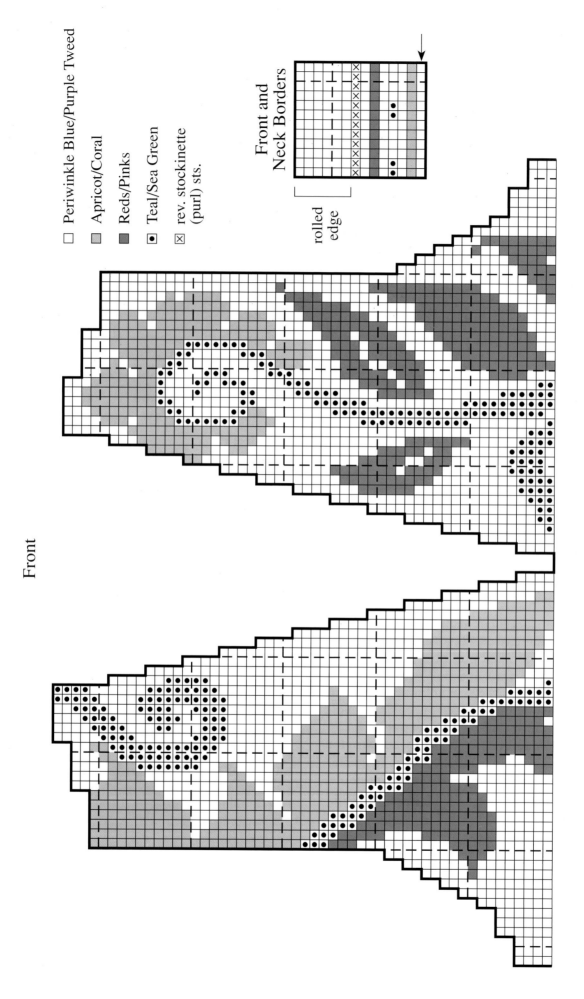

Lower Border

(first row is
decrease row)

hand knitters
begin here

machine knitters
begin here

Garden Exotica

Back

Legend:
- □ Periwinkle Blue/Purple Tweed
- ▨ Apricot/Coral
- ▨ Reds/Pinks
- ⊡ Teal/Sea Green
- ⊠ rev. stockinette (purl) sts.

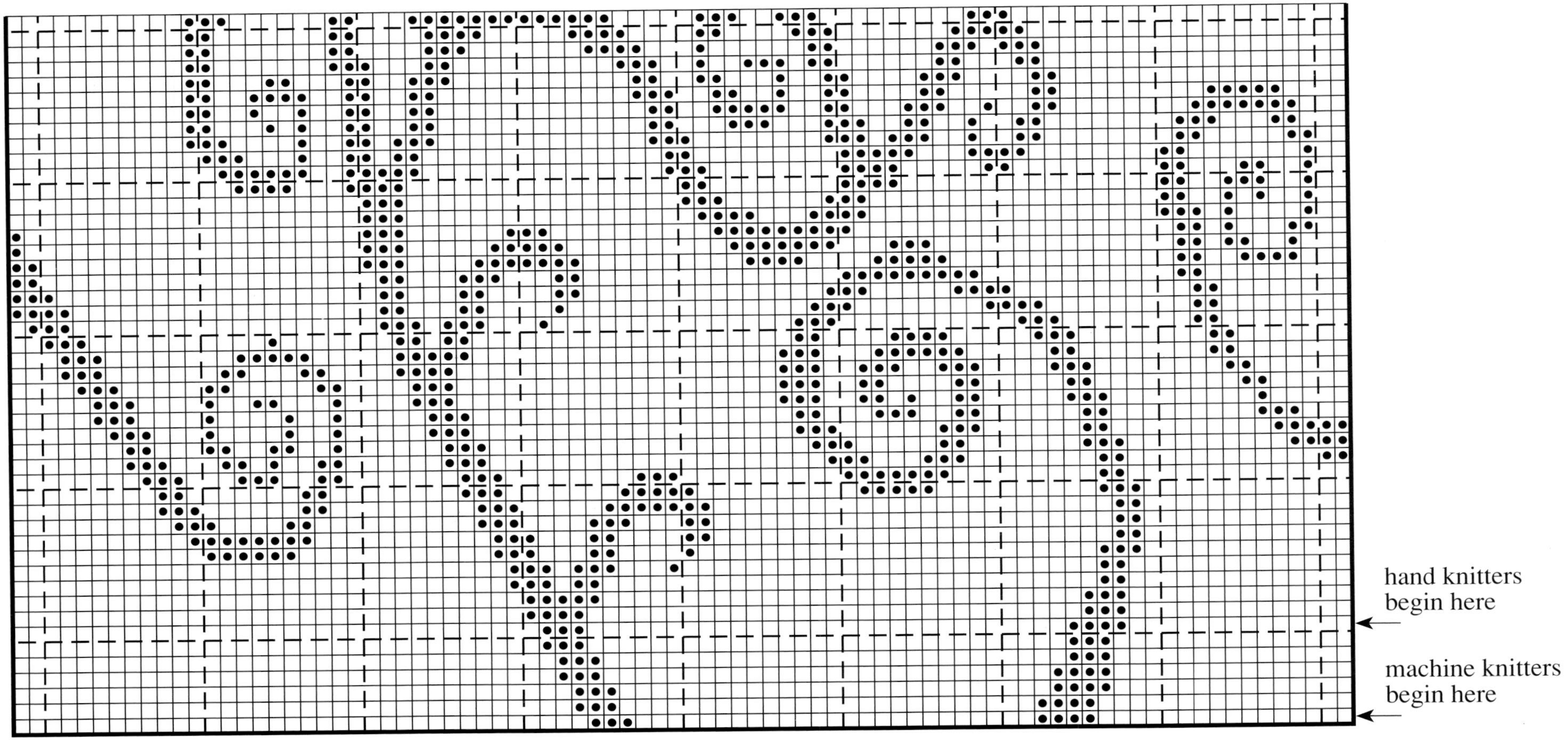

hand knitters
begin here

machine knitters
begin here

chart. Do not forget reverse stockinette stitch row for folded hem (pages 19–20). It is indicated on chart.

- When lower border chart is complete, attach background color and knit 14 more rows (or until lining is same depth as border.)
- Bring up first row of border and hang on needles. Change tension dial 2 settings higher and knit 1 row.
- Cast off. Slip stitch border edges together.

Front and Neck Border:

- *Hand knitters:* With smaller circular needle pick up 216 sts around neck in background color. Follow chart. Cast off.

- *Machine knitters:* If you do not choose to knit the front and neck border by hand, you will need to work in two sections on machine. Use a garter bar or small-gauge circular needle to remove and rehang knitting for reverse stockinette stitch. Follow chart. Cast off.

Finishing:

- Use crochet hook and single crochet to create 4 separate buttonhole loops on rolled edge of right front border. Weave in tails on inside of roll.
- Sew four ⅜-inch buttons on left side corresponding to button loops and centered on patterned part of border.

LEAPING CATS

Leaping Cats

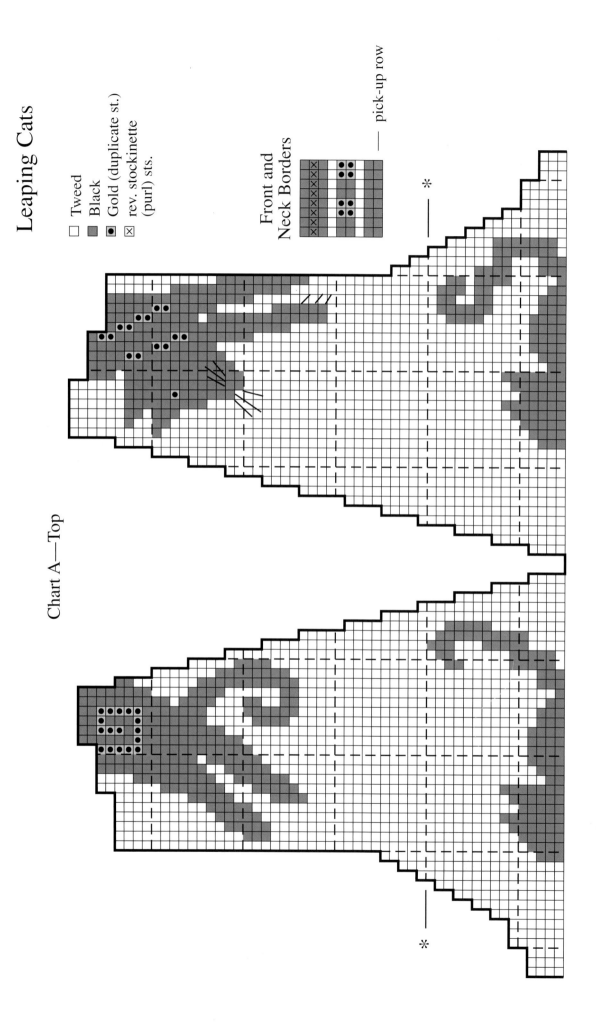

Chart A—Top

Legend:
- ☐ Tweed
- ▨ Black
- ⊡ Gold (duplicate st.)
- ⊠ rev. stockinette (purl) sts.

Front and Neck Borders

— pick-up row

*

reverse stockinette stitch row for folded hem (see pages 19–20). It is indicated on the chart.

▫ When lower border chart is complete, attach background color and knit 12 more rows (or until lining is same depth as border).

▫ Bring up first row of border sts and hang on needles. Change tension dial 2 settings higher and knit 1 row. Cast off. Slip stitch border edges together

Neck Edge: With smaller circular needle pick up 218 sts around neck in black (or your color choice).

▫ Follow chart for neck border.

▫ Finish lining in background color: 4 rows, or until depth of lining matches border.

▫ Fold border and use tapestry needle to attach to first row of border.

▫ *Machine Knitters:* If you choose to work the neck edge on machine rather than by hand, it will have to be knit in 2 sections. Using tension 4 or 5, follow chart for neck border, then work lining in background color to match depth of border. Hang hem, set tension dial 2 settings higher, knit one row. Cast off with tapestry needle.

RIOTOUS REINDEER

A felt appliqué rug made in the nineteenth century was the direct influence for the Riotous Reindeer sweater. I saw the rug in a wonderful book, *American Hooked and Sewn Rugs: Folk Art Underfoot*, by Joel and Kate Kopp. There are so many designs in this book to inspire

not only rug hookers, but also knitters, needle-workers, and artisans of all kinds.

It is nice to remember that the overwhelming majority of objects we admire from the past, be it quilts, rugs, pottery, weaving, or needlework, were made by ordinary people. Oh, some were artisans, but many of them were simply people who wanted to fancy up their homes, to make utilitarian objects that were pleasing to look at.

People the world over have always had an instinctive need to decorate. They did not go to art school to learn elements of design and color. They borrowed from each other, from illustrated books and fliers, from their surroundings, and came up with remarkably beautiful results. The tradition continues. . . .

I was instantly drawn to this particular rug not only by its simple and dramatic use of color, but also by the rug maker's random placement of the animal shapes and her charming disregard for their relative sizes. It gives the design a feeling that is at once primitive, irreverent, and a bit mysterious.

I hunted for many months for just the right red to use in this sweater. Many reds have too much orange in them. I wanted a red with just a touch of blue and vermilion—ruby red, alizarin crimson, cardinal red, the reds found in Navaho blankets and ethnic costumes from Eastern Europe to Asia. A Harrisville Designs' Twitchell Mills Tweed—Autumn Red—filled the requirements. It actually contains flecks of deep pink.

The red and black color scheme is very color saturated. When choosing a yarn for the yellow appliquéd eyes (it takes very little—you can use tapestry wool if you like), make sure it is a strong yellow/gold; pale yellow turns a spooky white, and lemon yellow looks sickly.

The sweater was knit as an oversized sweater for a rapidly growing adolescent. It fits a size 12 woman very comfortably. If you want to lengthen it, do so at the top, adding extra rows before starting neck shaping. I lengthened another version of this sweater by adding another Fair Isle motif to the border, thus doubling the depth of the border.

GAUGE

- Body: 16 stitches and 26 rows = 4 inches (4 sts and 6½ rows = 1 inch)
- Border: 4¼ sts and 6½ rows = 1 inch

This is a machine knit gauge. Hand knitters may find that they need fewer rows to achieve desired finished length. The best place to delete rows is at the bottom of the main body chart.

EQUIPMENT

- Size 8 or 9, 24-inch circular needle for body
- Size 6 or 7, 24-inch circular needle for borders
- Optional: 1 set size 6 or 7 double-pointed needles for seamless cuffs

(Adjust needle sizes as needed to achieve correct gauge.)

- Crochet hook, size F
- *Machine:* Large-gauge knitting machine set up for intarsia knitting
  Tension setting 8.5–9 for body
  Tension setting 7 for borders
  Tension setting 5 for linings

SUGGESTED YARNS AND NOTIONS

- 2 buttons (⅝-inch)
- Twitchell Mills Tweeds by Harrisville De-

signs: 5 skeins Autumn Red, 2 skeins Black. Equivalent yarn: Any yarn that has approximately 800 yds/lb, 10 WPI. Please read "Choosing Your Yarns," pages 13–15, if you plan to substitute yarns.

- 1 skein sport weight wool for linings—Black
- 1 oz yellow/gold yarn for appliqué
- Total sweater weight: 1.35 lbs

OVERALL MEASUREMENTS

- Total chest: 44 inches
- Body length: 23¾ inches (including 3-inch border)

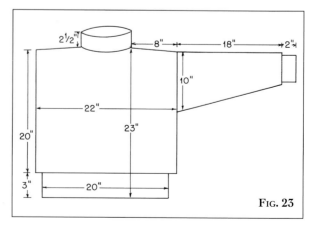

Fig. 23

INSTRUCTIONS

Note: The sweater in the photograph was knit by machine, so the motifs are the reverse image of the chart. Hand knitters will have a finished sweater with the same image as the chart.

Front or Back: With larger circular needle, or tension 8.5 or 9 for machine, cast on 88 sts using a simple cast-on, or cast on with waste yarn and pull cord (see page 17–19).

◻ Start chart at lower right-hand corner, attaching colors as indicated and securing tails as you knit (pages 23–25).

◻ Follow up the chart. Mark edge of sleeve openings with yarn markers where indicated on chart.

◻ Use short rows to shape neck and shoulders, front and back (pages 20–23).

◻ Put neck sts on holders or cast off with pull cord and waste yarn (page 18).

◻ *Hand knitters:* Cast off shoulders using regular cast-off method. This is a heavy sweater and benefits from being secured at the shoulders with a seam.

◻ *Machine knitters:* You may cast off with pull cord and waste yarn. Then hang shoulders front and back, right side together, on needles. Set tension dial 2 settings higher. Knit one row and cast off with tapestry needle.

◻ Check over all yarn tails to make sure they are secure. Trim tails to 1 inch.

◻ Gently wash and block sweater pieces as you complete them (especially machine knitters). (See pages 27–28.)

Sleeves: With larger needle, or main body tension setting on machine, cast on 54 sts in background color, using simple cast-on or universal cast-on for hand knit, and waste yarn/pull cord cast-on for machine.

◻ Follow chart, increasing 1 st at each edge every 8 rows. Use full-fashion increases (see page 26).

◻ When top of chart is reached, cast off using regular cast-off.

Neckband: Sew front and back together at right shoulder.

◻ Using smaller circular needle, or tension setting 7 on machine, pick up 78 sts around neck — all the sts on hold plus a couple of edge sts at shoulder.

◻ *Hand knitters:* Follow chart, knitting 2 rows of reverse stockinette stitch, then Fair Isle border.

◻ *Machine knitters:* Hang sts with right side of knitting facing you. Work 2 rows. Use garter bar to reverse knitting for Fair Isle part of border. Use garter bar to reverse knitting again at fold for hem (see pages 19–20).

◻ When border chart is complete, knit lining, using a lighter-weight wool. Knit to the same depth as the outside of neck border (approximately 11 rows, depending on yarn used).

◻ *Hand knitters:* Fold hem and secure last row of lining to first row of neckband with tapestry needle (page 20).

◻ *Machine knitters:* Take off lining sts with small-gauge circular needle. Use a tapestry needle to secure last row of lining sts to first row of neckband.

◻ Crochet 2 buttonhole loops in black to front edge of neckband opening at left shoulder, securing lining and right side of band. Slip stitch back edge of neckband to secure lining. Sew on 2 buttons.

Cuff Bands: Note: If using double-pointed needles to knit seamless cuff band, attach sleeves to body and sew underarm and side seams. Otherwise, pick up cuff sts before attaching sleeve. For either method, use size 6 or 7 needles.

◻ *Hand knitters:* Attach red yarn and knit 1 row,

Riotous Reindeer

□ Red
■ Black
☒ rev. stockinette (purl) sts.

Appliqué eyes and noses in yellow gold

Front and Back

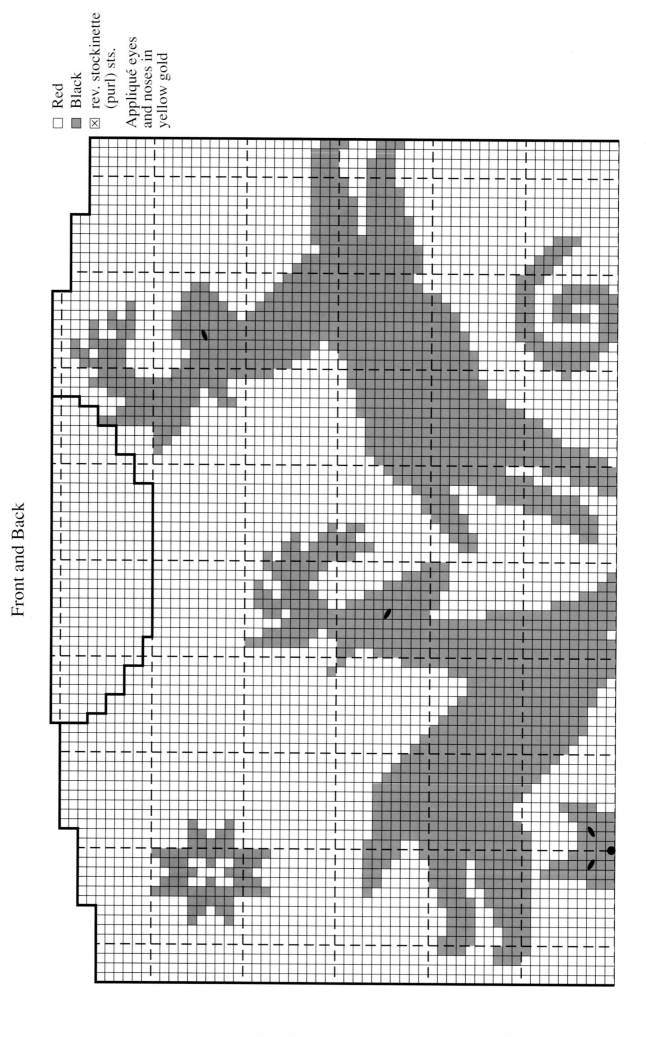

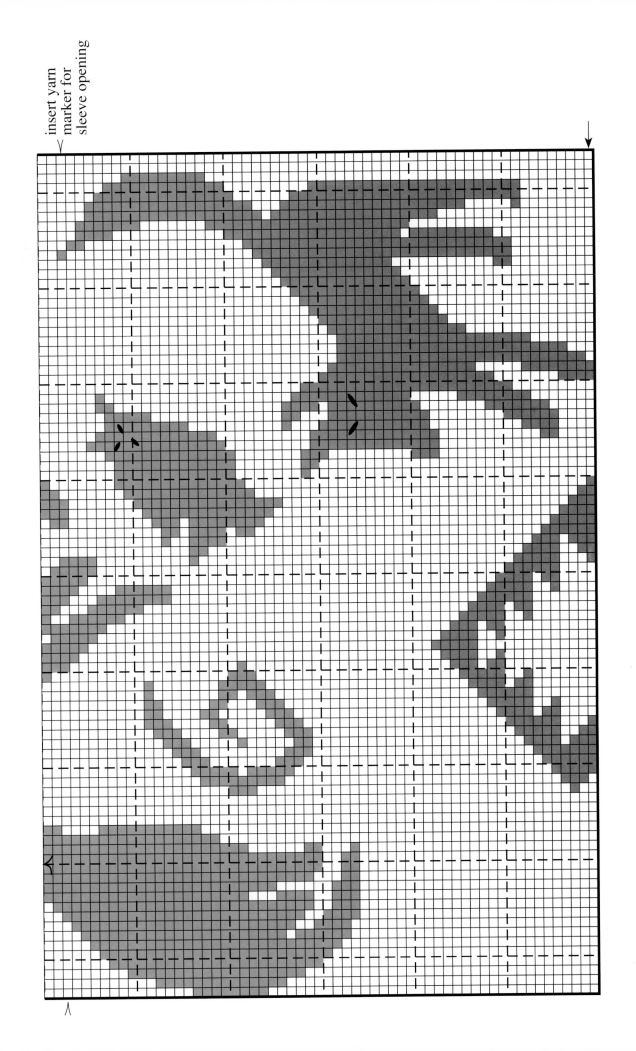

insert yarn
marker for
sleeve opening

Riotous Reindeer

Upper Sleeve

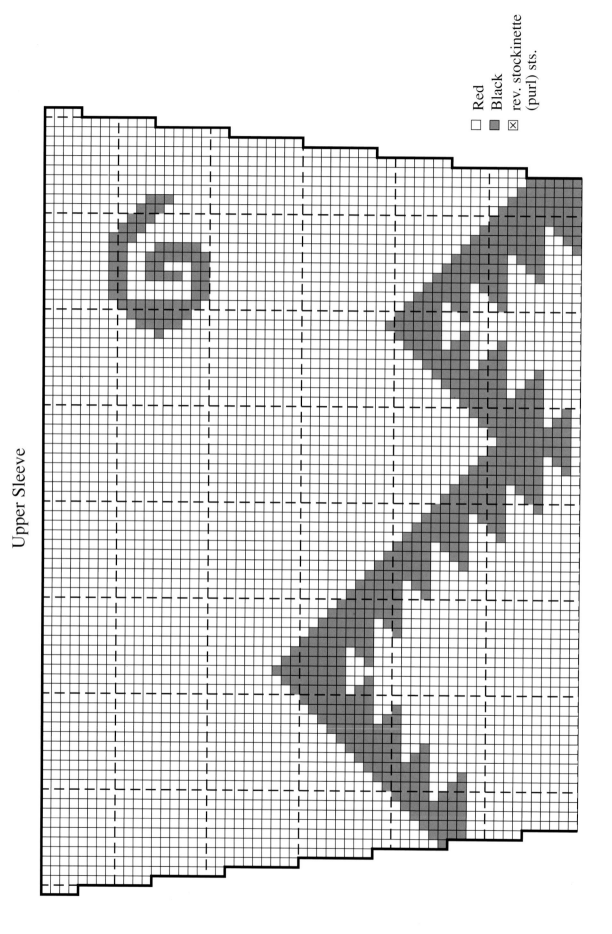

Red

Black

rev. stockinette
(purl) sts.

collar

cuff

Lower Sleeve

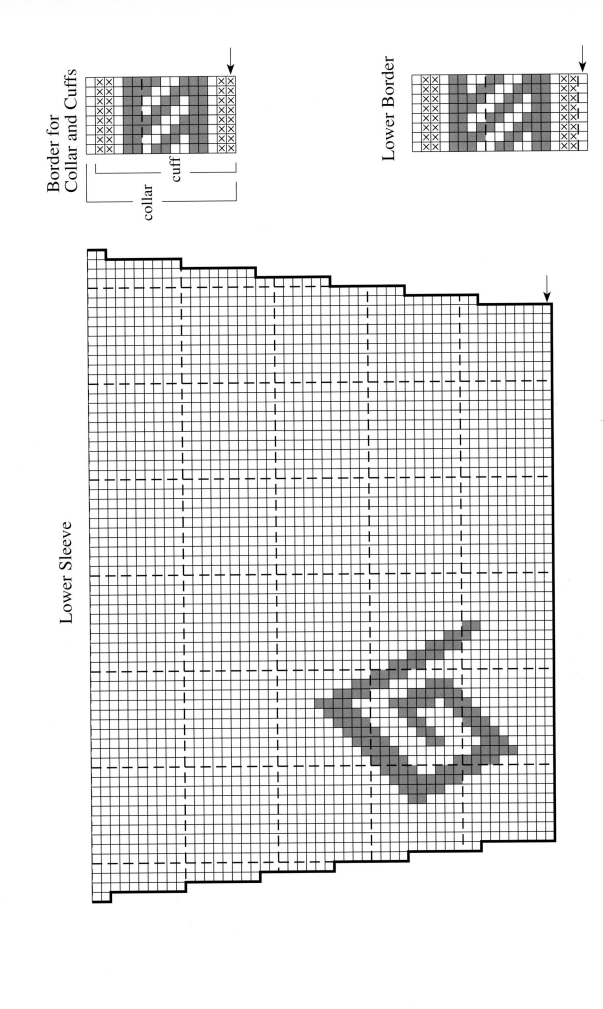

decreasing 18 sts. Knit 2 together every other st for a total of 36 sts.

- ◻ *Machine knitters:* Set tension dial at 7 and rehang lower edge of sleeve with 2 sts on every other needle, for a total of 36 sts. Work one row. Use garter bar to turn knitting for reverse stockinette stitch rows.
- ◻ Follow chart for cuff border.
- ◻ When complete, cast off firmly so edge will make a rolled hem.

Lower Border: (Machine knitters: If you want a seamless border, sew the side seams and knit the lower border by hand, as described below. For machine-knit border, knit border onto each piece *before* sewing the side seams.)

- ◻ After sleeves are attached and underarm and side seams are sewn, pick up all the sts around lower edge of front and back. Remove pull cord and waste yarn if you used them.
- ◻ Follow chart for lower band.
- ◻ When chart is complete, attach black and knit 11 rows. Cast off firmly and let this roll up to meet the two rows of reverse stockinette stitch

Gently hand wash and block sweater.

VICTORIAN FIRS

An antique Christmas stocking featured in a photo from a women's decorating magazine was the source for the Victorian Firs motif. For me, it evokes the magic of deep winter nights. There were no instructions for re-creating the stocking, so I used the photograph to create my own variation of the design.

That was a number of years ago, and the clipping has disappeared. I do not even remember whether the stocking was a knitting or cross-stitch design.

The first sweater I knit with this motif was a man's vest in Harrisville's sport weight Shetland Style wool, which was not a good choice for a strong black-and-white design. Shetland Style wool's special characteristic for blending and softening its appearance over time was in direct conflict with the crisp, clean nature of the black-and-white design. The vest is still around, but the white dots have all but disappeared and the firs are a dirty gray.

The friend who gave me the original magazine clipping needed a heavy, warm sweater for riding in winter. I decided to try the Victorian Firs again, this time using wools with a less fuzzy nature. Yarns with a smooth finish are best suited to designs where you want the motifs to maintain distinct outlines and colors. Many of the merino wools, cabled wools, and worsted-spun yarns would be suitable. (In worsted-spun yarns—not to be confused with worsted *weight*—the wool fibers are kept in parallel alignment during the spinning process, which yields a dense, smooth-surfaced yarn. For this pattern, avoid choosing woolen-spun yarns, where the fibers lie at mixed angles, resulting in a more fuzzy, fluffy, resilient yarn.) Check your local yarn store or write away to the yarn supply companies listed in the backs of most yarn and craft magazines. I have not been able to track down these kinds of yarns in heavy weights. They usually come in sport weight, which you can use doubled.

I used Halcyon Yarn's Victorian 2-ply (a sport weight yarn), with a merino wool that is no longer available. The Halcyon 2-ply doubled, or used with Jagger Spun Super Wash wool, would be good substitutions. Avoid blends with mohairs or alpacas, or wools that feel soft and fuzzy.

This sweater is best lengthened or shortened by adding or subtracting rows before working the armhole shaping. The chart was originally worked for knitting on machine, where the punch card automatically centers the design repeat on the sweater. Hand knitters please note the arrow that indicates where to begin working the chart in order to keep the motifs centered. If you plan to add or delete stitches to adjust the width of the sweater, do so from this arrow. Also bear in mind that if you change the sweater width, it will not be possible to keep the design continuous across the side seams.

GAUGE

□ Body: 16 sts and 23 rows = 4 inches (4 sts and 5¾ rows = 1 inch)
□ Borders: 4½ sts and 6 rows = 1 inch

Note: This is a machine knit gauge. Hand knitters should be sure to check their row gauge to determine whether to knit fewer rows to achieve desired finished length. The instructions give measurements for length of pieces as well as row counts (for machine knitters).

SUGGESTED NEEDLES/MACHINE TENSION

□ Size 7 or 8, 24-inch circular needle for body
□ Size 6 or 7, 24-inch circular needle for lower border
□ Optional: Size 6 or 7 double-pointed needles for seamless cuff and neck border
(Adjust needle sizes as needed to achieve correct gauge.)
□ *Machine:* Large-gauge machine set up for punch-card knitting
   Tension setting 7.5–8 for body and borders
   Tension setting 6 for border linings

SUGGESTED YARNS

One of the yarns used in the sweater in the photograph was a sport weight merino wool that is no longer available. Look for a yarn that knits up as a general worsted weight, either singly or when doubled, with 10 WPI. Keep in mind the high contrast and steer away from fuzzy yarns or Shetlands. Merinos, tapestry wool, and worsted wools are all suitable. Halcyon Yarn's Victorian 2-ply, doubled, would work well, as listed below:

   6 skeins Black (#134)
   4 skeins White (#103)
   2 skeins Red (#141)

"Choosing Your Yarns," pages 13–15, explains in detail about combining or substituting yarns.

OVERALL MEASUREMENTS

□ Total chest: 44 inches
□ Total length at shoulder: 24 inches (includes 2¼-inch border)
□ Total sleeve: 24 inches (includes 2¼-inch cuff border)

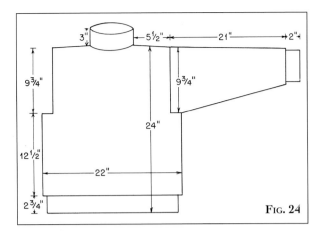

FIG. 24

INSTRUCTIONS

Front or Back: With larger circular needle, or 7.5–8 machine tension, cast on 96 sts. Use simple cast-on or universal cast-on for hand knit and waste yarn/ pull cord for machine (see pages 17 –19).

☐ *Hand knitters:* Start chart A in the center of the bottom row, at stitch 12, and repeat across. This way, the design will be centered on the sweater.

☐ *Machine knitters:* Punch a separate card of chart B, long enough to make a continuous card for your machine — 4 or 5 repeats.

☐ When chart A is complete, start chart B and continue on this chart until piece measures 12½ inches (71 rows for machine knitters).

☐ Cast off 9 sts at beginning of the next 2 rows for armholes.

☐ Continue in pattern until piece measures 19 inches (row 118 for machine knitters).

☐ Follow chart to shape neck openings and shoulders with short rows (see pages 20–23).

☐ Cast off neck sts with pull cord and waste yarn, or put on holders (page 18).

☐ *Hand knitters:* Cast off shoulder sts with regular cast-off. Sew right-hand shoulders together.

☐ *Machine knitters:* Cast off shoulder sts with pull cord and waste yarn. When front and back are complete, rehang right-hand shoulders together, right sides facing. Set tension dial 2 settings higher. Knit one row and cast off with tapestry needle.

☐ Gently wash and block pieces as you complete them (pages 27–28).

Neckband: With smaller circular needle, or tension 7.5 to 8 on machine, pick up 80 sts around neck — all sts on holders or waste yarn, plus a few edge sts at shoulders. Knit 1 row in red.

☐ Follow chart C for border. Machine knitters, use a garter bar for reverse stockinette stitch where indicated on chart (see pages 19–20).

☐ When chart is complete, knit lining in red — 15 rows.

☐ *Hand knitters:* To avoid a heavy seam at neck, use a tapestry needle to secure last row of lining sts to first row of border (see page 20).

☐ *Machine knitters:* Take lining sts off with small-gauge circular needle. Use a tapestry needle to secure last row of lining sts to first row of border (see page 20).

Sleeves: The sleeves are knit from the top down.

☐ *Hand knitters:* Using any method you like, cast on 84 sts.

☐ *Machine knitters:* Use any closed cast-on method to cast on 84 sts

☐ Follow lower section of chart A to marker. Change to chart B for the rest of the sleeve.

☐ At row 10, decrease 1 st at beginning and end of row, using full-fashion decreases (page 26).

☐ Continue to decrease 1 st at beginning and end of row, every 9 rows, 11 more times (until you have a total of 60 sts).

☐ Continue until sleeve measures 21¼ inches (124 rows for machine knitters).

☐ Gather sleeve for cuff. *Hand knitters:* Work first st singly, work 2 sts together across row, work last st singly. *Machine knitters:* Remove sleeve

Victorian Firs

☐ Black
■ White
▨ Red
☒ rev. stockinette (purl) sts.

Chart C:
Neckband

Chart D:
Cuff

Chart E:
Lower Border

Chart B:
Upper Body and
Lower Sleeve

top of
sleeve

Chart A:
Lower Body

hand knitters: begin working
design here and repeat across

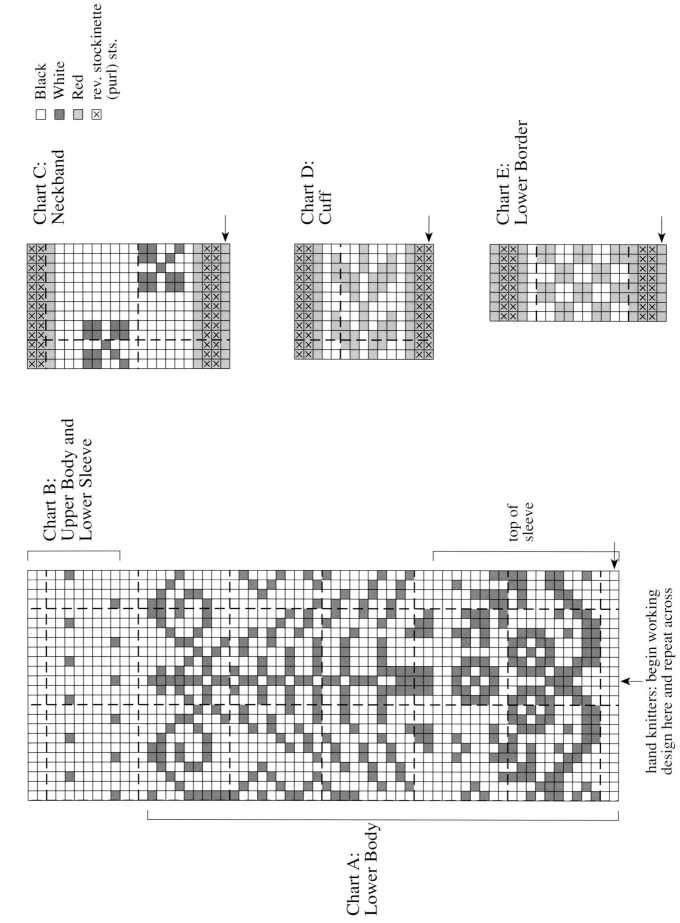

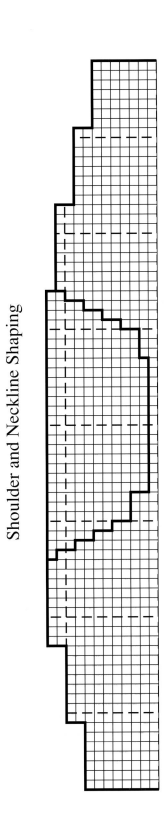

Shoulder and Neckline Shaping

sts from machine with small-gauge circular needle; rehang first and last sts singly, all other sts double, for a total of 31 sts.

⌑ Attach red and work 1 row.

Cuff Border: Note: If you want seamless cuffs, sew sleeve to shoulder, sew underarm seam, then work cuff chart on double-pointed needles. Otherwise work cuff before attaching to shoulder.

⌑ Follow chart D for cuff border. *Machine knitters:* Use garter bar to reverse knitting as indicated for reverse stockinette stitch rows.

⌑ Work lining in red, knitting 11 rows. Use a tapestry needle to secure last row of lining sts to first row of cuff border. Machine knitters can do this by taking off sts with small-gauge circular needle, then hemming.

⌑ If you worked the cuff borders flat, now sew sleeves to shoulder. Sew underarm seam.

Lower Border: (*Machine knitters:* If you want a seamless border, sew the side seams and knit the lower border by hand, as described below. For machine-knit border, knit border onto each piece *before* sewing the side seams.)

⌑ Pick up all the sts around lower edge on size 6 or 7 circular needle.

⌑ Remove pull cord and waste yarn if you used that cast-on method.

⌑ Knit 1 row of red.

⌑ Follow chart E for lower border. (*Machine knitters:* Use a garter bar to work rows of reverse stockinette stitch where indicated.)

⌑ After chart is complete, attach black and knit 14 rows for lining.

⌑ As for other borders, use a tapestry needle to secure last row of lining sts to first row of border.

If you did not block each piece of sweater as it was completed, gently hand wash and block sweater at this time.

FLORAL TAPESTRY

A beautiful silk scarf in a Metropolitan Museum of Art Christmas catalog inspired the colors and motifs for this floral tapestry. The arabesque leaf motifs are reminiscent of eight-eenth-century brocades. The florals are more contemporary—from my twentieth-century imagination.

I chose a very vibrant color scheme for a very vibrant woman, my mother-in-law. She loves flowers and fills her house with them year-round, making the most effortlessly beautiful flower arrangements I have ever seen.

The photograph was taken at Niagara Falls Conservatory in Canada. It is an exquisite place to spend a winter afternoon.

To try to duplicate this sweater exactly as I made it would be frustrating. It truly was a vehicle for using many, many different yarns. However, this design offers immense potential for exercising your own creativity. I chose a dark background full of rich tweeds to set off the florals. It would be equally handsome on solid black, or perhaps go to the opposite extreme and use a pale cream or pearl gray (gray with hints of lavender, pink, and blue) background. Mohair in the leaves and flowers softens the bright colors and makes them glow against the dark background.

There are many bulky weight yarns available, so you need not custom blend your own yarns if you do not want to. The chart presents the motifs in basic color groups. One skein for each color group, plus five or six skeins for the background would probably get you by. And you would have plenty left over for starting your own collection for future sweaters.

This is a roomy sweater that looks great on a wide range of body shapes. Because the motifs were laid out to exactly fill the sweater shape, I do not recommend trying to alter the size.

GAUGE

- Body: 15 stitches and 20 rows = 4 inches (3¾ sts and 5 rows = 1 inch)
- Borders: 4 sts and 6 rows = 1 inch

This is a hand knit gauge. Machine knitters may have to add rows to achieve desired finished body length. The chart indicates how machine knitters can add more rows at the bottom of the front and back pieces.

SUGGESTED NEEDLES / MACHINE TENSION

- Size 8 or 9, 24-inch circular needle for body
- Size 6 or 7, 24-inch circular needle for lower borders and collar
- Optional: Size 6 or 7 double-pointed needles for seamless cuff border
- Size 5, 24-inch circular needle for border linings (Adjust needle sizes as needed to achieve correct gauge.)
- Size F crochet hook
- *Machine:* Large-gauge knitting machine set for intarsia knitting
  Tension setting 8–8.5 for body
  Tension setting 7 for cuffs and border
  Tension setting 5 for linings

SUGGESTED YARNS AND NOTIONS

- 3 buttons (⅝-inch)
- Bulky-weight yarns, or combinations of lighter yarns to knit up equivalent to bulky yarn, totaling about 1 lb 12 oz (10 WPI, 600 to 900 yds/lb).
- Allow approximately 1 lb for background color.
- Allow approximately 12 oz total for floral and leaf motifs. Individual flower motifs may use only ½ to 1 oz, or 10 to 20 yds each. Leaf motifs may take closer to 2 oz.
- Border lining: One 3½-oz skein wool sport weight yarn.
- Yarn combinations in the sweater shown include: Halcyon Yarn's sport weight Victorian 2-ply, mohairs, and Scottish tapestry wools; Harrisville Designs' sport weight Shetland Style and 2-ply Tweeds; Jagger Spun Maine Line wool 2/20s; various bits of rayon/acrylic/wool novelty blends, and sport weight cotton chenille.
- A detailed list of yarns and colors used appears on page 118. "Choosing Your Yarns," pages 13–15, explains in detail about combining or substituting yarns.

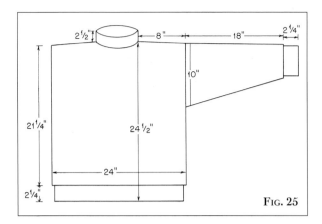

FIG. 25

OVERALL MEASUREMENTS

▯ Total chest: 48 inches
▯ Total length from shoulder: 24½ inches (includes 2¼-inch border)
▯ Total sleeve: 21½ inches (includes 2¼-inch cuff border)

INSTRUCTIONS

Note: The sweater in the photo was hand knit, so machine knitters will have the reverse image on their finished sweater.

Front or Back: With size 8 or 9 needles, or tension 8–8.5 for machine, cast on 88 sts using waste yarn and pull cord, or simple cast-on (see pages 17–19). (Waste yarn and pull cord method is recommended.) Start chart at lower right-hand corner with a knit row, attaching colors as indicated and securing tails as you knit (pages 23–25).
▯ Follow up chart. Mark sleeve opening with

yarn marker where indicated. Use short rows (pages 20–23) to shape neck, front, and back. Put neck stitches on holders or cast off with pull cord and waste yarn (page 18). Cast off shoulders using a regular cast-off method; this is a heavy sweater and benefits from being secured at the shoulders with a seam.
▯ Check over all yarn tails to make sure they are secure. Trim tails to 1 inch. Gently wash and block sweater pieces as you complete them (pages 27–28).

Sleeves: With larger needles, or main body tension on machine, cast on 42 sts in background color, using simple cast-on for hand knit, waste yarn and pull cord cast on for machine knit.
▯ Follow chart, increasing 1 st at each edge every 4 rows. (Use full-fashion increases, page 26.)
▯ If using custom blended yarns for the background, vary their lengths, or use two or three lengths in a random zigzag pattern to keep a nice variation going, until floral and leaf motif is reached.
▯ When chart is complete, cast off using regular cast-off.

Neckband: Sew front and back together at the right shoulder.
▯ Using size 6 or 7 circular needle, or tension 7 on machine, pick up 68 sts around neck—all the sts on hold, plus 2 edge sts at shoulders.
▯ Follow chart for neck border. Machine knitters: Use a garter bar to reverse knitting to create 1 row of reverse stockinette stitch for fold of band (pages 19–20).
▯ When chart is complete, knit lining, using size 5 circular needle, or tension 5 for machine, and sport weight yarn. Knit to same depth as the outside of neck border (approximately 14 rows, depending on yarn used).
▯ *Hand knitters:* Fold hem and use a tapestry needle to secure last row of lining to first row of neckband (see page 20).
▯ *Machine knitters:* Bring up first row of neckband and hang on needles. Change tension dial 2 settings higher and knit 1 row. Cast off.
▯ Crochet 3 button loops in background color to front edge of neckband opening, securing lining to right side of band. Slip stitch back edge of band to secure lining. Sew on 3 buttons.

Floral Tapestry

Front and Back

yarn
marker

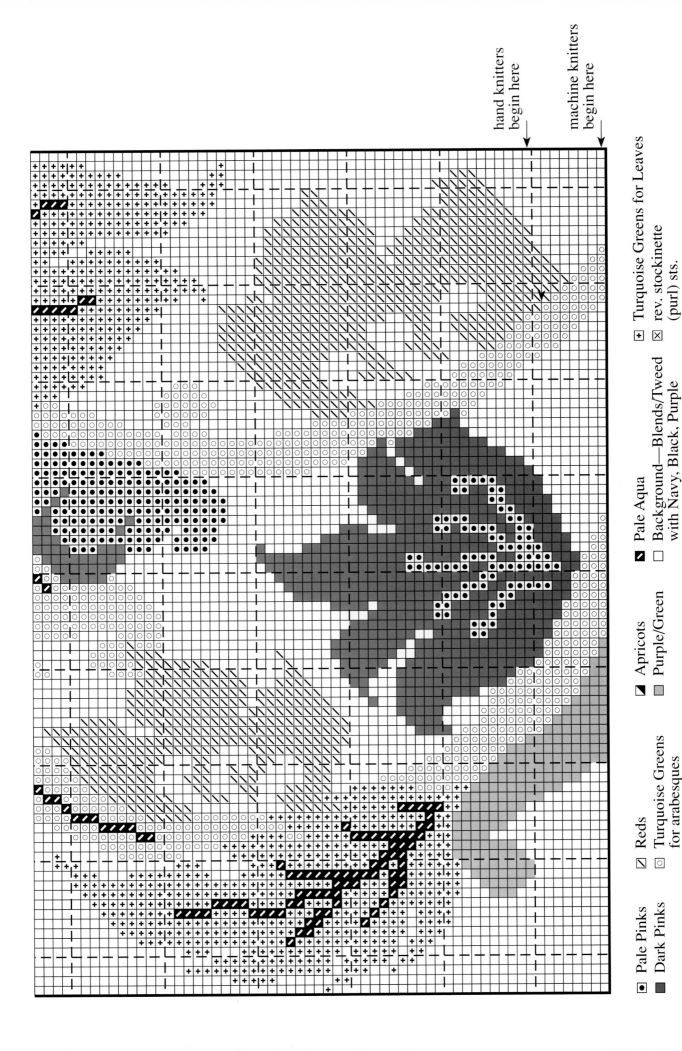

hand knitters
begin here

machine knitters
begin here

- ⊞ Pale Pinks
- ■ Dark Pinks
- ◪ Reds
- ⊡ Turquoise Greens for arabesques
- ◢ Apricots
- ■ Purple/Green
- ⊞ Pale Aqua
- ☐ Background—Blends/Tweed with Navy, Black, Purple
- ⊞ Turquoise Greens for Leaves
- ⊠ rev. stockinette (purl) sts.

Floral Tapestry

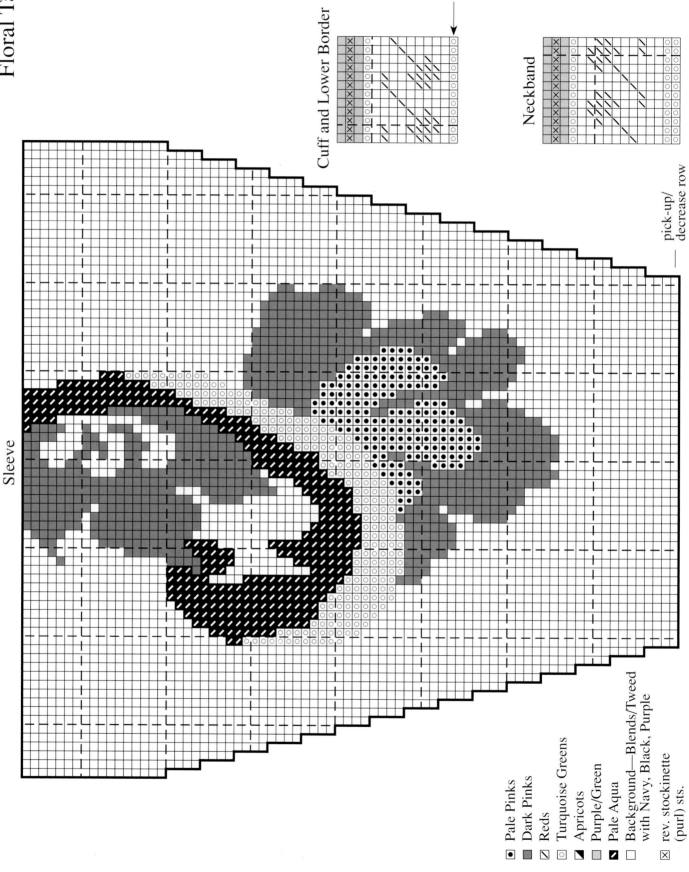

Cuff and Lower Border

Neckband

Sleeve

— pick-up/
decrease row

- ● Pale Pinks
- ▨ Dark Pinks
- ◪ Reds
- ⊙ Turquoise Greens
- ◣ Apricots
- ▨ Purple/Green
- ◪ Pale Aqua
- ☐ Background—Blends/Tweed
  with Navy, Black, Purple
- ☒ rev. stockinette
  (purl) sts.

Cuff Borders: Note: If using double-pointed needles to knit seamless cuffs, first attach sleeves to body and sew underarm and side seams. Otherwise, pick up cuff stitches before attaching sleeve. For either method use size 6 or 7 needles.

- Attach contrast yarn and knit first row of cuff chart, decreasing 10 sts—knit 2 together every third st, for a total of 32 sts.
- *Machine knitters:* Set tension dial to 7 and rehang lower edge of sleeve with 2 sts on every third needle, for a total of 32 needles.
- Follow chart for cuff border.
- When chart is complete, attach sport weight yarn. Using size 5 needles, or tension 5 on machine, knit cuff lining to same depth as outside border (approximately 12 rows).
- *Hand knitters:* Fold hem and use tapestry needle to secure last row of stitches to first row of cuff.
- *Machine knitters:* Bring up first row of cuff and hang on needles. Knit 1 row with tension dial set 2 numbers higher. Cast off.

Lower Border: (Machine knitters: If you want a seamless border, sew the side seams and knit the lower border by hand, as described below. For machine-knit border, knit border onto each piece *before* sewing the side seams.)

- After sleeve is attached and underarm and side seam are sewn, pick up all the stitches around lower edge of front and back. Remove pull cord and waste yarn.
- Using size 6 or 7 circular needle, or tension 7 on machine, work chart for lower band.
- Attach sport weight yarn, change to smaller needle (tension 5 on machine), and knit lining (approximately 12 rows).
- *Hand knitters:* Use tapestry needle to secure last row of stitches to first row of border.
- *Machine knitters:* Bring first row of border up and hang on needles. Knit 1 row with tension dial set 2 numbers higher. Cast off.

If you did not wash each sweater piece as it was completed, gently hand wash and block sweater.

ORIENTAL MOTIF

The house where we live in the winter has been occupied since the 1830s. The land has been used for many centuries. Although there is scarcely any evidence of the indigenous people's use of this site, evidence of nineteenth-century settlers abounds.

My favorite spot to look for bits and pieces of old treasure is the little shingle beach down below the boat workshop. After every storm, polished and worn bits of glass and old crockery surface amongst the shells and gravel. Their colors are stained by rust and bleached by sun. One can only imagine their original shape and use.

This house was one of the original inns on Casco Bay, so the plates and crockery were abundant, and probably not of great value. Given its history, my imagination was excited by the thought of seafaring folk returning from the China trade with the plates, cups, and serving bowls of which these bits and pieces were once a part.

A wonderful book, *The Grammar of Chinese Ornament*, by Owen Jones, also contributed to the design of this sweater. The book was originally published in 1867 and influenced many graphic artists and designers in the nineteenth century, including William Morris. It was recently republished by Crown Publishers. It is filled with 100 meticulous reproductions of decorations from Chinese vases, bowls, jars, plates, and bottles. As a source for decorative borders, it is unequaled.

The gauge for this sweater is worsted weight. It is basically a 2-color Fair Isle design with a 24-stitch repeat. The rows never repeat themselves, so if you are knitting it on a machine, the punch card will be at least 120 rows long. I say "at least" because machine knitters may need to add up to 8 more rows to achieve the same final length as on the original hand-knit version. See note under "Gauge" below.

Even if you knit the body and sleeves by machine, the borders are best knit by hand. The cuff and lower borders are 22-stitch repeats.

I gathered up all my natural whites, beiges, palest grays and blue heathers for the background. I used cobalt blues, blue heathers, teal blue, periwinkle blue, navy blue, and just a bit of forest green in the foreground pattern. The borders have stripes of coral and motifs in Oriental jade green. *The Grammar of Chinese Ornament* also offers many beautiful and unusual Oriental color schemes to consider, if you want to try a different combination from the one shown here.

The yarns are all sport weight used double. You could easily substitute worsted weight tweeds or heathers, if you are not inclined toward blending your own yarns. Be careful when substituting tweeds, however; any tweed used in the pale background should be subtly colored—Harrisville Designs' Wildflower Tweed, for example.

This is a roomy, long sweater. If you want to shorten it, do so at the bottom of the chart.

GAUGE

- Body: 18 sts and 21 rows = 4 inches (4½ sts and 5¼ rows = 1 inch)
- Borders: 4½ sts and 6½ rows = 1 inch

This is a hand knit gauge. Machine knitters may have to knit more rows to achieve desired body length. Extra rows have been added to the bottom of the chart for this purpose.

EQUIPMENT

- Size 7 or 8, 24-inch circular needle for body
- Size 5, 24-inch circular needle for borders, cuffs, and neckband
- Optional: Size 5 double-pointed needles for seamless cuff

(Adjust needle sizes as needed to achieve correct gauge.)
- Machine: Large-gauge machine with punch card capacity
  Tension 7–8 for body
  Tension 5.5–6 for borders

SUGGESTED YARNS

Multiple-plied yarns that knit up as slightly heavy worsted weight (800 to 900 yds per lb, 11 WPI) or compatible worsted weight yarns. "Choosing Your Yarns," pages 13–15, explains in detail about combining or substituting yarns.
- Total weight of sweater: 2 lbs
- Background: 1 lb (color A)

□ Body motifs and collar background: 1 lb (color B)

□ Small amounts, approximately 2 oz each, of coral/pink (color C) and jade green (color D) for border motifs

□ Lining: 3½ oz skein of sport weight yarn

The yarn combinations I used included: Halcyon Yarn's sport weight Victorian 2-ply and mohair; Harrisville Designs' 1-ply Tweeds and sport weight Shetland Style; Jagger Spun Maine Line 2/8s; and odd bits of alpaca, thin cotton bouclé, and silk/alpaca blend. A detailed yarn list can be found on pages 118–119.

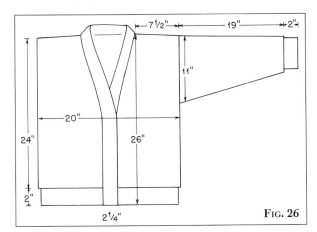

FIG. 26

OVERALL MEASUREMENTS

□ Total chest: 40 inches
□ Total length: 26 inches (includes 2-inch border)
□ Sleeve: 21 inches (with 2-inch cuff)

INSTRUCTIONS

Back: With larger circular needle or machine tension 7–8, cast on 88 sts using waste yarn/ pull cord method (page 17–18).

□ Start chart at lower right-hand corner. This is a 24-stitch repeat. Continue up chart, placing yarn markers where indicated for sleeve placement.

□ When you reach top of chart, divide knitting into shoulder sections of 29 sts and neck section of 30 sts. Knit off each section onto pull cord/ waste yarn (page 18).

Fronts: It is helpful to knit both fronts at the same time so front neck shaping is identical and pattern is continuous.

□ Cast on 44 sts for each front, using waste yarn/ pull cord method.

□ Start chart at lower right-hand corner.

□ Continue up chart. Start shaping of front neck on row indicated.

□ Using full-fashion decreases (page 26), decrease 1 st at neck edge every 6 rows 6 times, then every 4 rows 9 times. Continue on 29 sts to top of chart. (Note: You may find it helpful to take a colored pencil and mark these decreases where they will occur on the chart. After you knit the fronts, erase the marks, then you can mark decreases for the sleeve shaping. Another option is to make photocopies and mark on those.)

□ Mark sleeve placement with yarn markers where indicated.

□ When top of chart is reached, knit off shoulder onto pull cord/waste yarn.

□ Graft shoulders together using invisible grafting technique (page 19).

Sleeves: Sleeves are knit from the top down.

□ *Hand knitters:* With motif yarn (blues), pick up 96 sts on shoulder between yarn markers.

□ *Machine knitters:* With wrong side facing you, hang bars of shoulder sts between markers on 96 needles. Work 1 row in motif yarn (blues).

□ Follow chart *from the top down*.

□ Work 6 rows on 96 sts.

□ Using full-fashion decreases, decrease 1 st at beginning and end of row 7.

□ Continue down chart, decreasing 2 sts as above every 5 rows until 60 sts remain.

□ When the last row marked for sleeve is complete, work 1 row in background color A and decrease for cuff. *Hand knitters:* Knit 1, knit 2 tog across row, knit last st. If you reach this row and it is a purl row, then work decreases as purl sts. *Machine knitters:* Take knitting off machine and rehang on 31 needles.

Cuff: Work the cuff by hand, even if body of sweater was machine knit. If you want a seamless cuff, sew underarm and side seam together and work in the round on double-pointed needles. To work the cuff flat, leave sleeve seam open and change to needles indicated for cuffs.
- Follow chart for cuff. The design is a 22-stitch repeat.
- When chart is complete, attach lining yarn and knit lining to same depth as cuff.
- Use a tapestry needle to secure each lining st to first row of cuff (page 20).

Lower Border: Work the lower border by hand.
- Sew underarm and side seams if you have not already done so.
- With circular needle indicated for borders, pick up 176 sts around bottom of sweater. Remove pull cord/waste yarn (page 18).
- Attach color C and knit first row of chart,

decreasing 20 sts evenly spaced (approximately every 8 sts). Continue working on 156 sts.
- When chart is complete, attach lining yarn and knit lining to same depth as border.
- Secure last row of lining sts to first row of border with a tapestry needle.

Front Opening and Neckband: (If you have a 36-inch circular needle in the correct size, you can work this band in 1 piece. If not, work in 2 sections from center back, as described below.)
- With color C, and needle size indicated for borders, pick up 132 sts on right front from center back to end of lower border.
- Knit chart. The pattern is a 24-stitch repeat.
- When chart is complete, change to lining yarn and knit lining to same depth as border.
- Cast off.
- Repeat for left front, picking up 132 sts from lower border to center back.
- Start chart where indicated for left side so your pattern will be continuous.
- When cast-off is complete, sew center back seam. Then hem cast-off row of lining to first row of border.

Gently wash and block sweater (pages 27–28).

Oriental Motif

Neckband and Front Border

pick-up row

Cuff and Lower Border

Main Body (upper portion) Sleeve (from shoulder)

insert yarn marker for sleeve opening

begin sleeve (turn chart 180°)

begin decrease for neck opening this row

- ■ Blue
- □ Off White
- ▨ Coral
- ⊙ Jade
- ⊠ rev. stockinette (purl) sts.

begin body

extra rows for machine knitters

Main Body (lower portion) Sleeve (to cuff)

end sleeve

DAYLILIES

The daylilies in our island gardens seem to keep the looming firs that cover the rest of the island at bay. Their brilliant yellow blossoms look spectacular against the deep filtered light of the woods.

The first Daylily sweater I attempted was such a complex pattern of flowers and crisscrossed leaves covering the entire sweater that I was overwhelmed. The resulting knitted piece was more confusing than interesting.

A look at a pastel I had recently completed with the same daylilies gave me the inspiration I needed to refine the design. By utilizing the dense woods as a backdrop and limiting the daylilies and their crossed leaves to the lower half of the sweater, the composition suddenly took on a very dramatic feel.

I chose Jagger Spun's Maine Line 2/8 wools (fingering weight) to knit this design because their very smooth finish keeps the composition crisp. Shetland Style wools would not be appropriate, as their main purpose is to blend. The yarns are thin, so I used them doubled. They have an exquisite feel—like the old-fashioned layette wools you cannot find anymore.

The smoothness of the Jagger Spun wool and the high contrast between motifs and background on this sweater make the weaving in of yarn tails undesirable (except where a color can be woven back on itself) because the woven tails will show through on the right side of the knitting. I used a tapestry needle to tie half hitches for each tail as I knit.

A gentle reminder: Do not leave finishing off of tails to the last on these sweaters. The task would be overwhelming, and the sweater would probably spend the rest of its life in the knitting basket. Secure the tails as you work. An alternative would be to work on tails every few rows, so the task would seem less disruptive to the knitting process.

This sweater is a comfortable medium—size 10 to 12. It is a medium length, so if you desire a longer sweater, add rows in the upper half where there are no flowers. If you look carefully at the chart, you will notice that the diagonal streaks in the background colors are very regular. They advance across the sweater one stitch at a time, so you could add rows here with very little difficulty.

GAUGE

- Body: 21 sts and 29 rows = 4 inches (5¼ sts and 7¼ rows = 1 inch)
- Borders: 5½ sts and 7¼ rows = 1 inch

This is a machine knit gauge. Hand knitters may find that they knit fewer rows per inch. It would probably only amount to 1 to 1½ inches over the total length of this sweater. You may delete rows in the upper midsection without much trouble. The diagonal stripes in the background advance very regularly.

EQUIPMENT

- Size 5 or 6, 24-inch circular needle for body and borders
- Size 4, 24-inch circular needle for border linings
- Optional: 1 set each of sizes 4 and 6 double-pointed needles for seamless cuff and neck borders

(Adjust needle sizes as needed to achieve correct gauge.)

- Machine: Large-gauge machine set up for intarsia

Tension setting 4.5 for both body and borders. Note: Although I knit this sweater on a large-gauge machine, the yarn and gauge may be better suited to a mid-range or standard-gauge machine. The large-gauge machine really stretches the yarn across the needles, so it is imperative to wash and block all sweater pieces (see page 27).

SUGGESTED YARNS

- Jagger Spun Maine Line 2/8 knit double—available on 275-yd (1.96 oz) mini cones (2240 yds/lb; when knit double: 1120 yds/lb, 13 WPI).
- 2 cones each of the following colors:
    #23—Marigold
    #34—Mint
    #25—Daffodil
    #37—Teal
    #33—Jade
    #53—Turquoise

□ 3 cones each of the following colors:
  #32 — Capri Green
  #35 — Peacock
  #39 — Marine Blue

Equivalent yarns: Any yarn that yields the same gauge. To keep the overall design crisp, look for merino or worsted wools. Stay away from Shetland Style, unless you desire the design to blend and fuzz. "Choosing Your Yarns," pages 13–15, explains in detail about combining or substituting yarns.

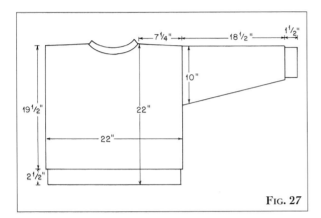

FIG. 27

OVERALL MEASUREMENTS

□ Total chest: 44 inches
□ Total length at shoulder: 22 inches (includes 2¼-inch border)
□ Total sleeve: 20 inches (includes 1¾-inch border)

INSTRUCTIONS

Note: Since the sweater in the photograph was knit by machine, the design on the finished sweater is the reverse of the design on the chart. A hand knit sweater will be the same image as on the chart.

□ Prepare several bobbins or butterflies (page 25) of each color combination. The background combinations are used frequently, so it is good to have 8 or 10 lengths handy. Use them randomly, since they are so close in color value, to simulate shadowy foliage.

Front or Back: With needles/machine tension indicated for main tension, cast on 110 sts with waste yarn and pull cord (page 17–18).

□ Begin chart from lower right-hand corner, attaching yarns as indicated, securing tails as you knit (page 24).
□ Mark sleeve opening with yarn marker where indicated on chart.
□ Follow chart to neck and shoulder shaping. Use short rows to shape neck and shoulders (pages 20–23).
□ Cast off neck and shoulder sts onto pull cord/waste yarn (page 18).

Sleeves: With needles/machine tension indicated for body, cast on 52 sts with waste yarn and pull cord.

□ Begin chart from lower right-hand corner, attaching yarns as indicated, securing tails as you knit.
□ Knit 4 rows. Increase 1 st at beginning and end of next row, using full-fashion increases (page 26).
□ Continue following chart, making increases every 5 rows until you have 100 sts
□ Cast off with regular cast-off when you reach top of sleeve.

Neckband: Graft right shoulder using invisible grafting technique (page 19). (If you will be working a seamless neck border on double-pointed needles, graft *both* shoulders before picking up sts.)

□ Remove pull cord and waste yarn.
□ With background yarn, pick up 90 sts around neck with needles/machine tension indicated: 84 sts from pull cord/waste yarn plus 3 edge sts on each shoulder.
□ Work section of chart marked for neck.
□ Attach background yarn and work 1 row of

Daylilies

Front and Back

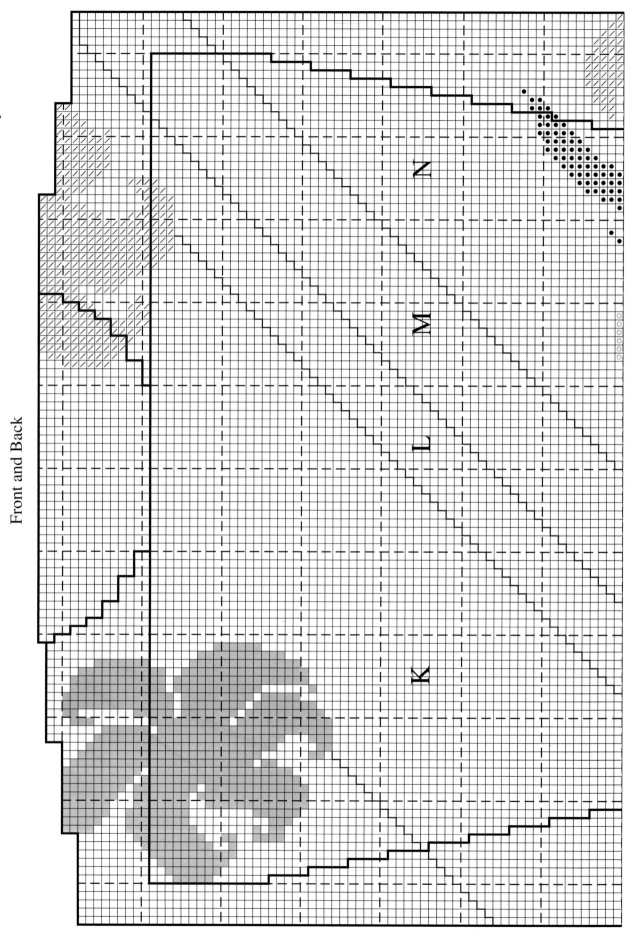

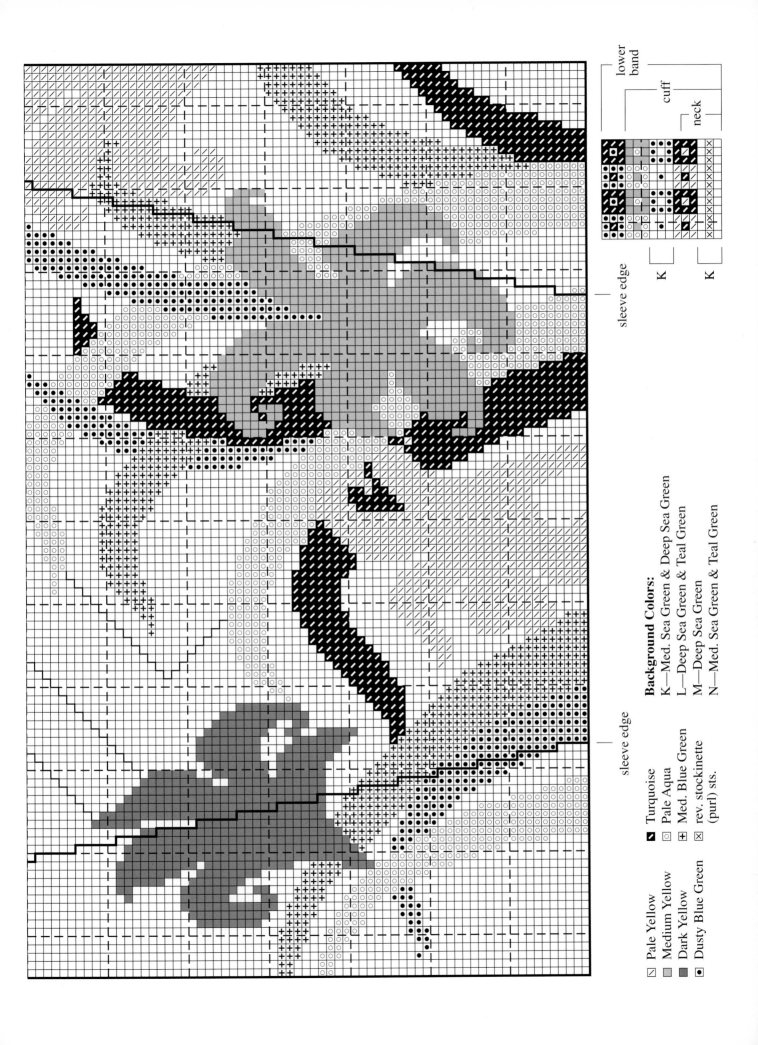

Background Colors:
K—Med. Sea Green & Deep Sea Green
L—Deep Sea Green & Teal Green
M—Deep Sea Green
N—Med. Sea Green & Teal Green

◩ Pale Yellow   ◼ Turquoise
▨ Medium Yellow   ⊙ Pale Aqua
▩ Dark Yellow   ⊞ Med. Blue Green
• Dusty Blue Green   ⊠ rev. stockinette (purl) sts.

lower band
cuff
neck
sleeve edge
sleeve edge
K
K

stockinette stitch, 2 rows of reverse stockinette stitch. Machine knitters: Use a garter bar to reverse knitting for reverse stockinette stitch rows (pages 19–20).

◻ Change to smaller needles/machine tension and work 5 rows of stockinette stitch for lining.

◻ *Hand knitters:* Secure lining sts to first row of border with a tapestry needle (page 20).

◻ *Machine knitters:* Take off lining sts with a small-gauge circular needle. Use a tapestry needle to secure last row of lining sts to first row of border (see page 20).

Cuff Borders: (If working seamless borders with double-pointed needles, attach sleeves to body, and sew underarm and side seams before working cuffs. To work the cuff borders flat, knit cuffs before attaching sleeves to body.)

◻ With needles/machine tension indicated, pick up 52 sts on bottom of sleeve and remove waste yarn/pull cord.

◻ With background color, knit first row of chart, decreasing 10 sts evenly, approximately every fifth st. Cuff is worked on 42 sts.

◻ Follow chart for rows marked for cuff.

◻ Attach background color, work 1 row stockinette stitch, 2 rows reverse stockinette stitch. *Machine knitters:* Use a garter bar or small-gauge circular needle to remove and rehang knitting.

◻ Change to smaller needles/machine tension and work 12 rows for lining. Secure lining using same technique as for neckband.

Lower Border: *Machine knitters:* If you choose to knit the border by machine, do so before sewing up side seams. Work border on 108 sts; hang 2 sts together at each edge, all the rest singly.

◻ To work a seamless border by hand, with larger circular needle pick up lower edge sts.

◻ Remove waste yarn/pull cord.

◻ Attach background yarn and begin lower border chart, decreasing 2 sts at each side seam. Lower border is worked on a total of 216 sts.

◻ When lower border is finished, attach background yarn and work 1 row of stockinette stitch, 1 row of reverse stockinette stitch, and 3 more rows of stockinette stitch.

◻ Cast off with a nice even cast-off and let the last few rows form a rolled edge.

Floral Patchwork

This sweater was designed for a friend who is a star gardener. She has shared so much over the years, from seedlings and perennial divisions to a wealth of information on gardening.

The body of the sweater is worked in patchwork squares. It is a nice way to experiment with blending and stranding yarns yet not be overwhelmed. You can concentrate on the flowers individually. Since the squares are small—29 stitches by 40 rows, mistakes or unpleasing combinations are easily unraveled. I knit the back with 4 floral squares and 5 plain squares, but feel free to make your own arrangement.

This is a real scrap bag sweater—the only purchases necessary when I made the original were extra blues and grays used in the background and sleeves. You might consider soft beiges and off-whites for a background. Or perhaps a combination of navy blues, blacks, and the darkest of purples—either would be very elegant and set off the flowers well.

Making this sweater would be a great opportunity to pool resources with other knitters. They could supply their own preferred background yarns and share yarns for the flowers. The flowers take very little yarn. They get their richness from a wide variety of blends. The charts are coded in simple color shades, e.g., light pink, medium pink, dark pink. Depending on the yarns you have available, you can make your own variations.

An extensive list of the yarns I used in this sweater is given at the back of the book (pages 119–120). As I try to emphasize for all the sweaters using blended yarns, you can interpret the charts more simply and substitute other yarns locally available to you. Just make sure they knit up to a comparable gauge.

The Floral Patchwork was designed to be a roomy size 12. It would be easy to size the sweater smaller or larger. By adding 1 stitch to the edges of each square, you could increase the overall size by nearly 4 inches in total width and 1½ inches in length. By reducing each square by 1 stitch all around, you can similarly decrease the size. You could also just add or subtract 1 stitch per square for less dramatic increases or decreases.

The sweaters in this book are a challenge, but beyond that, they are fun to knit, and you will be so proud when you have completed one!

GAUGE

- Body: 15 sts and 21 rows = 4 inches (3¾ sts and 5¼ rows = 1 inch)
- Borders: 4 sts and 6 rows = 1 inch

Note: This is the hand knit gauge. Machine knitters may find that their 4-inch test swatch runs to more than 21 rows, and they might have to add 2 or 3 rows per patchwork square in order to achieve the desired length.

EQUIPMENT

- Size 8 or 9, 16-inch circular needle for squares
- Size 6, 24-inch circular needle for lower border and neck
- Optional: Size 6 double-pointed needles for seamless cuff
- Size 4, 24-inch circular needle for border linings

(Adjust needle sizes as needed to achieve correct gauge.)

- Size H crochet hook
- Machine: Large-gauge machine set up for intarsia knitting
  Tension setting 8.5–9 for squares
  Tension setting 6.5–7 for borders
  Tension setting 5 for linings

SUGGESTED YARNS AND NOTIONS

- 3 buttons for neck closure (½-inch)
- Halcyon Yarn's sport weight Victorian, mohairs, pearl cottons, pearl silks, Scottish tapestry wool, and loopy mohair. Harrisville Designs' sport weight Shetland Style. Jagger Spun 2/8 Maine Line Wool (fingering weight). Reynolds worsted-weight yarn, and Kitten. Brown Sheep Wool/Mohair blend. Various bits of cotton chenille, rayon/silk blend, and novelty cotton/rayon/acrylic blends.
- "Choosing your Yarns," pages 13–15, explains in detail about combining or substituting yarns.

- Yarns are used in combinations that will yield the above gauge (approximately 600 to 900 yds/lb, 10 WPI).
- Total weight: 1 lb, 14 oz
- Background yarns totaling 1 lb, 4 oz
- Flowers and leaves: small amounts, 1 to 2 oz for each color group
- Linings for neck and lower border: 1 mini cone each of Jagger Spun 2/8 Maine Line Wool in colors #48—Cobalt, and #55—Iris
- Lining for cuffs: 1 mini cone each of Jagger Spun 2/8 Maine Line Wool in colors #—32 Capri Green and #53—Turquoise green

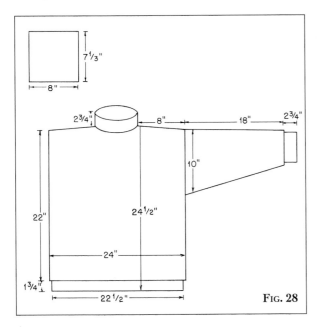

FIG. 28

OVERALL MEASUREMENTS

- Total chest: 48 inches
- Total body length: 25¼ inches (includes 1¾-inch border)
- Total sleeve: 20¾ inches (includes 2¾-inch border)

INSTRUCTIONS

Note: The sweater in the photograph was knit by hand. Machine knitters will end up with the reverse image on their finished sweater.

Patchwork Squares: Both hand and machine knitters may use waste yarn/pull cord cast-on (page 17) for the bottom 3 squares so the stitches are easily picked up for knitting the border. Use simple closed cast-on for the rest of the squares.
- Using larger circular needle, or machine tension 8.5 or 9, cast on 29 sts using simple cast-on, changing yarns as indicated on charts.
- Knit 40 rows, following the color changes indicated on the charts.
- The last row of the chart is your cast-off row. Use a regular cast-off.
- For the top-row "squares," use short rows to shape necks and shoulders (pages 20–23) as indicated on the charts.
- Cast off necks onto pull cord/waste yarn or put on holders (page 18). Cast off shoulders using regular cast-off.
- Check all tails to make sure they are secured (pages 23–25). Trim to 1 inch. Gently hand wash and block each piece as you finish — especially machine-knit pieces (pages 27–28).

Sleeves: Sleeves are knit from the shoulder down. With larger circular needle, or 8.5–9 machine tension, cast on 70 sts using any closed cast-on method.
- Knit in stockinette stitch for 14 rows.
- Decrease 1 st at beginning and end of next row, using full-fashion decrease (page 26).
- Continue decreasing every 10 rows until you have a total of 56 sts.
- Continue until sleeve measures 16 inches — approximately 95 rows on machine — or desired length.
- *Hand knitters:* Knit 1, knit 2 together across — sts reduced to 37 for cuff.
- *Machine knitters:* Take knitting off machine and rehang, alternating 1 st, 2 sts together across — 37 needles total.

Cuff Border: (If you wish to knit a seamless cuff border, slip sts onto a length of yarn or transfer to 3 double-pointed needles. Assemble sweater first and knit borders by hand. Otherwise, proceed with the cuff borders after finishing sleeve decreases.)

▫ Change to needles/machine tension indicated for borders.

▫ Change to contrast yarn and follow chart for cuff border.

▫ *Machine knitters:* Use a garter bar or small-gauge circular needle to remove and rehang knitting for the reverse stockinette stitch row (pages 19–20).

▫ Change to lining yarn and needles/machine tension indicated. Knit lining to same depth as cuff border (approximately 17 rows).

▫ *Hand knitters:* Fold hem and secure last row of lining sts to first row of border using a tapestry needle (see page 20).

▫ *Machine knitters:* Bring up first row of border and hang on needles with lining. Change tension 2 settings higher. Work 1 row. Cast off using a tapestry needle cast-off.

Assembling the Sweater: Arrange patches in order. Using crochet hook and 2 sport weight strands in background color, single crochet vertical edges of patches where they meet, with wrong sides together so crocheted edge is on right side of sweater.

▫ Crochet the 3 patch strips together.

▫ Crochet right shoulders together.

▫ Pick up neck sts on needles/machine tension indicated for borders—68 sts total, all sts on pull cord/waste yarn, plus 3 edge sts at shoulders. Remove waste yarn.

▫ Follow chart for neckband.

▫ Change to needle/machine tension indicated for lining, attach lining yarn and knit lining to same depth as neckband (approximately 17 rows).

▫ *Hand knitters:* Hem by securing each lining st to first row of border with a tapestry needle.

▫ *Machine knitters:* Bring up first row of border and hang on needles with lining. Set tension 2 settings higher. Knit 1 row. Cast off with a tapestry needle.

▫ Crochet left shoulder.

▫ Crochet button loops to front edge of neckband opening, securing lining and front of border edge.

▫ Slip stitch back edge of band together and sew on buttons.

▫ Sew sleeves to body between markers. Sew underarm seam on sleeves.

Lower Border: For machine-knit borders, work border on front and back pieces before sewing side seams. Rehang each piece on 84 needles.

▫ For a seamless hand-knit border, sew side seams, then pick up 174 sts around lower edge of sweater with needles indicated for border. Attach contrast yarn, work first row of chart, decreasing 6 sts evenly spaced, for a total of 168 sts.

▫ Work remaining rows of chart.

▫ Using needles/machine tension indicated, attach lining yarn and knit lining to same depth as border, approximately 12 rows. Hem the same as other borders.

Floral Patchwork

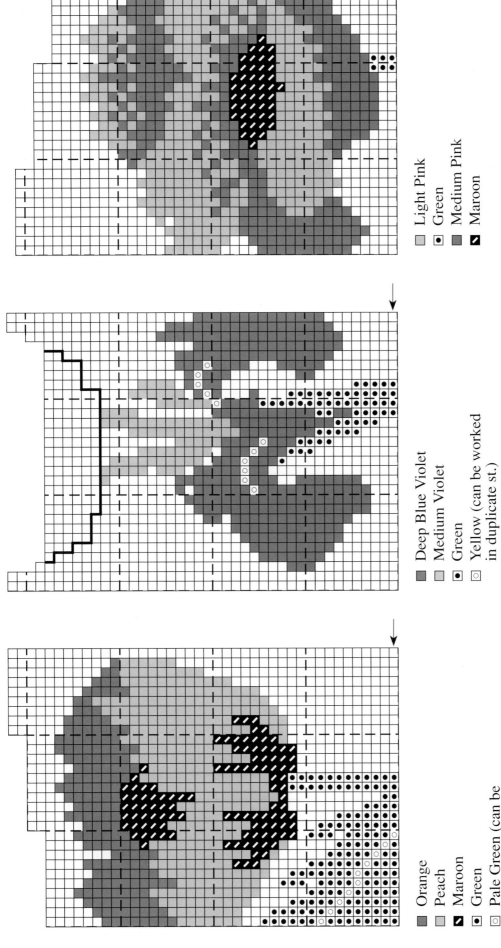

Orange
Peach
Maroon
Green
Pale Green (can be worked in duplicate st.)

Deep Blue Violet
Medium Violet
Green
Yellow (can be worked in duplicate st.)

Light Pink
Green
Medium Pink
Maroon

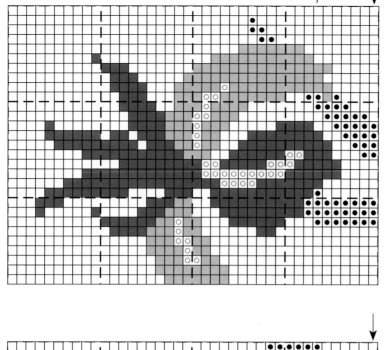

■ Deep Blue/Violet

■ Medium Violet

⊡ Green

⊙ Yellow (can be worked
   in duplicate stitch)

↽ insert yarn marker
   for sleeve opening

■ Deep Red

■ Red Orange

⊡ Green

◪ Maroon

⊙ Pale Orange (can be worked
   in duplicate stitch)

■ Deep Blue/Violet

■ Pale Lavender/Blue

⊡ Green

⊙ Yellow (can be worked
   in duplicate stitch)

Floral Patchwork

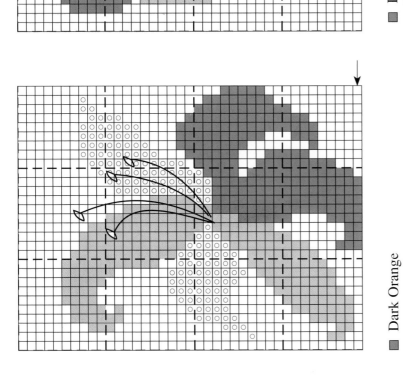

Pale Yellow
- Green
- Bright Yellow

chain st. flower stamens in yellow

Lower Band

- Green
- Purple

× rev. stockinette (purl) sts.

■ Dark Pink
□ Light Pink
- Green
▨ Medium Pink

flower stamens: chain st. filaments in gold, anthers in bronze

■ Dark Orange
□ Light Orange
○ Medium Orange

chain st. flower stamens in Deep Bronze

Neckband and Cuffs

- Green
- Purple

× rev. stockinette (purl) sts.

OAK LEAVES

Photographed in front of an Assyrian wall relief, 883–859 B.C. • *Bowdoin College Museum of Art, Brunswick, Maine.*

OAK LEAVES

Fallen leaves on a rain-soaked road, in puddles and ponds. . . .
Their momentary brilliance shimmers against dark reflective surfaces.

A friend gave me the pearl silks found in these leaf motifs as a present—an extravagant gift! I hoarded them for a couple of years, reluctant to dip into their jewel-like colors.

They also presented a technical problem: Pearl silks have absolutely no elasticity. In hand-knitting gauges, they do not keep their shape, and sweaters made exclusively of silk will grow and grow. I do not know how machine-knit fabrics and sweaters of impossibly tiny gauges overcome this trait, but they do.

By using wool with silk, I hoped to overcome the elasticity problem. I did not want to blend the silks with wool; instead, I wanted the design to allow for the wool to travel across the entire sweater, lending its support to the silk. The leaf design provided the solution, because the leaf *veins* are knit with wool. Although each leaf is knit as a separate color motif in pearl silks, the wool continues across the knitting. For each leaf, you are working with one ball of background color, and one length of leaf color(s) wound into butterflies or onto bobbins (as described on page 25). It is a combination of Fair Isle and intarsia knitting. Descriptions always make it seem more complicated than it is in practice.

I am not sure how this sweater would knit up by machine. Therefore, I am not including machine directions. If you are an adventurous machine knitter, however, give it a try.

The background is knit with one strand sport weight wool and one strand of 5/2 pearl cotton. I wanted the black to have a slight sheen—suggestive of reflective surfaces.

This is a comfortable vest that fits nicely on sizes 8 to 12. To make a larger size, you could add stitches at the sides. (Cast off the added stitches at the armhole marker so the shoulders do not get too wide.) To lengthen, add plain rows at the bottom of the sweater. Making this sweater smaller would be difficult because of the design. You could try knitting with smaller needles in a tighter gauge to reduce the overall dimensions

If you choose to knit this design in all wool, make sure you knit a gauge swatch. It is very likely that you will have more rows per inch in your swatch and will have to adjust the pattern by adding rows at the bottom of the chart. The wool/silk combination I used still stretched slightly, making for an odd gauge.

There are many options besides silk for the leaf motif and borders. A highly textured yarn, blends of rayon/silk/wool, or slightly fuzzy yarns in fall colors could be equally interesting. How about cotton chenille . . . now there is an idea worth pursuing.

GAUGE

- Body: 22 sts and 24 rows = 4 inches (5½ sts and 6 rows = 1 inch)
- Border: 5½ sts and 7 rows = 1 inch

SUGGESTED NEEDLES

- Size 5 or 6, 24-inch circular needle for body
- Size 3 or 4, 24-inch circular needle for neck and lower borders
- Size 2 needles for lining and armhole hem

Adjust needle sizes as needed to achieve correct gauge.

SUGGESTED YARNS

- Background: 1 strand Jagger Spun 3/8 Super Wash wool knit with 1 strand 5/2 pearl cotton (knits up at 1800 yds/lb, 14 WPI)
- 5 mini cones Jagger Spun 3/8 Super Wash wool in Black (1490 yds/lb)
- 5 mini cones Halcyon Yarn 5/2 pearl cotton in Black (2000 yds/lb)
- Leaf motifs and borders: Halcyon Yarn 2/12 pearl silks, knit in 3-strand combinations. These silks run 3300 yds/lb; when used tripled, 952 yds/lb and 14 WPI.

□ 3 mini cones (205 yds per cone) each of following colors:

#1 Amber
#2 Tiger's Eye
#3 Jacinth
#5 Coral
#6 Pale Ruby
#7 Rose Jade
#9 Lilac Quartz
#12 Sapphire
#13 Mother of Pearl

Equivalent yarns: Any yarns that knit up to required gauge and have 14 WPI. Yards per pound will vary greatly when using silks or cottons with wools. You might substitute 3 strands of 10/2 pearl cotton for the silk for economy's sake. For the background, you could use any sport weight 2-ply wool, merino or worsted, with a fingering weight cotton. "Choosing Your Yarns," pages 13–15 explains in detail about combining or substituting yarns.

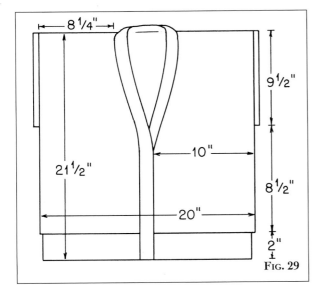

FIG. 29

OVERALL MEASUREMENTS

□ Total chest: 40 inches
□ Total length at shoulder: 21½ inches (includes 2¼-inch border)

INSTRUCTIONS

Back: With needles indicated for body, cast on 106 sts with simple or universal cast-on (pages 18–19).

□ Follow chart, placing yarn markers where indicated for side seam.
□ Shape shoulders using short rows (pages 20–23). Cast off shoulder sts onto pull cord and waste yarn (page 18).
□ Put neck sts on holder or cast off onto pull cord/waste yarn.
□ Gently wash, spin dry, and block each sweater piece as it's finished (pages 27–28).

Front: With needles indicated for main tension, cast on 50 sts using same cast-on as for back.

□ Follow chart, placing yarn marker where indicated for side seam.
□ Use full-fashion decreases for neck shaping (page 26). Delete the central motif where it appears at the neck edge on the chart—just knit background color here on sweater fronts.
□ Shape shoulders the same as for back, casting off with pull cord/waste yarn.

Armhole Edging: Graft shoulders together with invisible grafting technique (page 19).

□ With background yarn and size 2 needles, pick up 94 sts around armhole. Knit 1 row.
□ Change to contrast yarn. Knit 5 rows of stockinette stitch, purl side to the outside. Cast off and let hem roll to the inside.

Oak Leaves

Front and Back

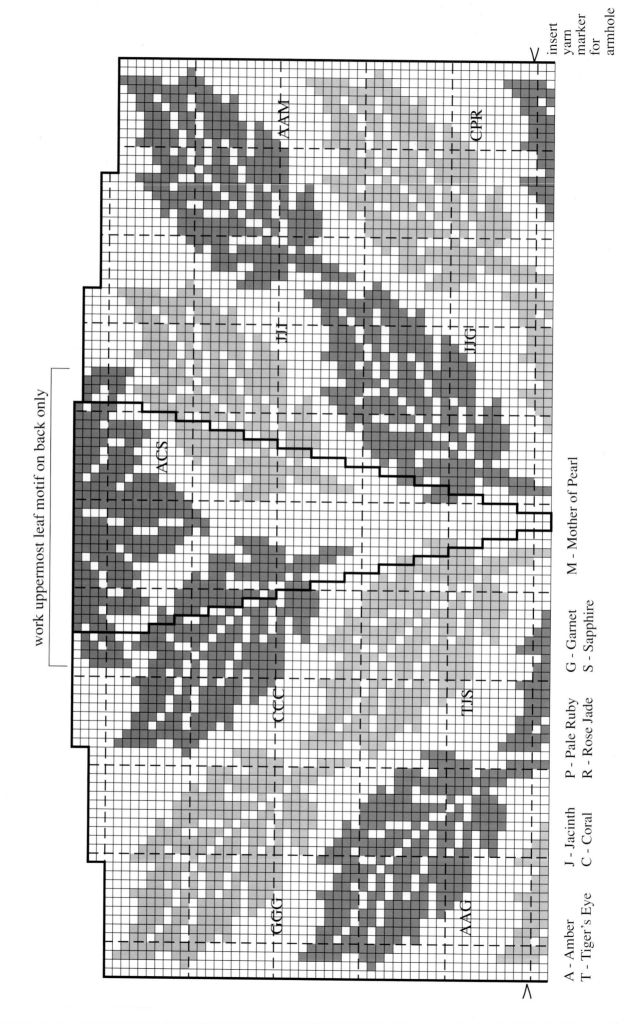

work uppermost leaf motif on back only

ACS

AAM

CPR

TJT

JJG

GGG

CCC

TJS

AAG

insert yarn marker for armhole

A - Amber   J - Jacinth   P - Pale Ruby   G - Garnet   M - Mother of Pearl
T - Tiger's Eye   C - Coral   R - Rose Jade   S - Sapphire

center front

Neckline and Center Front Edge

Lower Border

Note: Abreviations in capital letters stand for the 3-strand blends for each leaf motif. Example: GGP = 2 strands Garnet, 1 strand Pale Ruby.

A - Amber
T - Tigers Eye
J - Jacinth
C - Coral
P - Pale Ruby
R - Rose Jade
G - Garnet
S - Sapphire
M - Mother of Pearl

☐ Mother of Pearl
⊡ Black
☐ Sapphire

■ Lilac Quartz
⊠ rev. stockinette (purl) sts.

Lower Border: Sew side seam, including armhole edging.

- With needles indicated for lower border, pick up 206 sts around lower border.
- Attach contrast yarn and follow chart B.
- When chart is complete, change to size 2 needles and background yarn.
- Knit lining to same depth as border—approximately 15 rows.
- Fold border and secure last row of lining to first row of border with a tapestry needle (page 20).

Border for Neck and Front Edges: With needles indicated for borders and black yarn, pick up 244 sts around entire neck edge. (You may knit neck border in two sections of 122 sts each, if you prefer.)

- Follow chart C for border.
- When chart is complete, change to size 2 needles and black yarn.
- Knit lining to same depth as border.
- Cast off, fold, and sew edge of lining to first row of border.

Yarn Lists

The following yarn lists are included to identify the specific yarns used in the sweaters made with doubled and tripled yarns in custom color combinations. Because these sweaters represent five years of knitting, some of the yarns I used are no longer available. Some yarn companies change their colors and yarn styles yearly, others far less frequently. Many of the novelty yarns are not carefully identified because I lost their tags long ago or bought them as close-outs.

I encourage you to use the following lists as a jumping-off point—to pursue your own yarn sources, your own color combinations. Each of these sweaters is open to personal interpretation, so go to it—experiment. There will be no "knit by numbers" for these sweaters!

In the "Choosing Your Yarns" chapter, pages 13 to 15, you will find useful tables comparing all the various yarn weights available and listing different yarn combinations that all yield a comparable gauge when knit.

Good yarn stores seem to be getting scarce as the years go by, so support your local yarn stores. Some will special order yarns from manufacturers they don't usually carry, and a knowledgeable yarn shop manager can be very helpful for suggesting alternative yarns.

To mail order many of the yarns used in these sweaters:

> **Halcyon Yarn**
> **12 School St.**
> **Bath, ME 04530**

For a list of retail suppliers for Harrisville Designs Shetland Style and Tweeds:

> **Harrisville Designs**
> **Center Village**
> **Box 806**
> **Harrisville, NH 03450**

Abbreviations Used in Yarn Lists

F   fingering weight
S   sport weight
F/S between fingering and sport weight
W   worsted weight
B   bulky weight
W/B between worsted and bulky
N/A Yarn no longer available (*Not to worry; there are plenty of comparable yarns out there for substitution.*)

Note: I have used the manufacturers' color designations where available, capitalized (e.g., Midnight Blue). In some cases, the colors are identified by number. Colors not capitalized (pale blue, for example) are my descriptive names used where the manufacturer has not supplied an official color label.

SEASHELLS YARN LIST

Background Yellows
Lopi Icelandic (B): pale yellow
Jagger Spun 2/8 Maine Line Wool (F): #25 Daffodil, #24 Chrome
Halcyon Yarn 2/5 Pearl Silk (S) N/A: palest yellow
Halcyon Yarn Mohair (W): #103 off-white
Halcyon Yarn Lollipop cotton/rayon (W): #113 pale yellow
Halcyon Yarn Scottish Tapestry Wool (W/B): #108 yellow
Shetland-type wool yarn (F) N/A: yellow/beige
1-ply angora/silk (S) N/A: off-white
cotton bouclé (S) N/A: off-white

Shell/Starfish — Coral and Apricot Shades
Halcyon Yarn Victorian 2-ply Wool (S): #109 peach

Halcyon Yarn 5/2 Pearl Cotton (F/S): #118 coral

Halcyon Yarn 2/12 Pearl Silk (F) used double: #5 coral, #6 pale ruby

Jagger Spun 2/8 Maine Line Wool (F): #27 Apricot, #26 Watermelon

Reynolds Kitten wool/acrylic (W): palest peach

novelty yarns in cotton/acrylic/rayon: coral, peach, and pink

Harrisville Designs Shetland Style Wool (F/S): Orange Peel, Aster, Orange/Beige N/A, Pale Peach N/A

Shells and Border — Blues and Grays
Halcyon Yarn Victorian 2-ply Wool (S): #125 dark blue, #126 navy

Halcyon Yarn 5/2 Pearl Cottons (F/S): #129 lavender, #154 pale blue, #157 cobalt

Halcyon Yarn Lollipop cotton/rayon (W): #126 cobalt

Halycon Yarn 2/12 Pearl Silk (F): #12 Midnight Blue

Halcyon Yarn Mohair (W): #123 periwinkle

Harrisville Designs 1-ply Wool (F): Dawn Mist

Harrisville Designs Shetland Style Wool (F/S): Cornflower, Wedgwood, Periwinkle, Aubergine, Gray/Blue N/A, Navy, Lilac, Blueberry

Harrisville Designs 2-ply Tweed (W): Dawn Mist, True Blue, Indigo

Seaweeds
Elite Specialty Yarn, 25% silk/75% rayon (W): rainbow-dyed sea green, teal, maroon, bittersweet, and purple

Jagger Spun 2/8 Maine Line Wool (F): #32 Capri Green, #35 Peacock

Halcyon Yarn Victorian 2-ply Wool (S): #123 teal, #130 pale sea green, #117 maroon, #125 smoky blue

DARK/LIGHT SEA DUCKS YARN LIST

Light Colors
Halcyon Yarn Victorian 2-ply Wool (S): #103 white, #104 natural

Jagger Spun 2/8 Maine Line Wool (F): #8 Shale

Jagger Spun 3/8 Super Wash Wool (S): #9 Pewter

Reynolds Kitten, wool/acrylic (W): #206 natural

Halcyon Yarn Mohair (W): #103 white

Harrisville Designs 1-ply Tweed (F): Wild Flower

Harrisville Designs Shetland Style Wool (F/S): Pearl, Sand, Silver Mauve

Harrisville Designs Trillium, cotton/wool (F) N/A: pale beige/pale sea green

Halcyon Yarn Cotton Bouclé (S): #30 natural

Halcyon Yarn Wool/Angora N/A: #190 off-white

Dark Colors
Halcyon Yarn Victorian 2-ply Wool (S): #125 deep periwinkle, #126 navy, #133 forest green, #128 deep teal

Harrisville Designs Shetland Style Wool (F/S): Hemlock, Woodsmoke, Cobalt, Blackberry, Evergreen, Aqua Blue, Royal, Navy, Aubergine, Loden Blue, Cornflower

Harrisville Designs 2-ply Tweed (W): Indigo, True Blue

Tipperary Tweed (B) N/A: navy, deep teal green

Red Accent
Halcyon Yarn Victorian 2-ply Wool (S): #141 Red

Harrisville Designs Shetland Style Wool (F/S): Blackberry

Linings of Borders
Jagger Spun 2/8 Maine Line Wool (F): #42 Admiral Blue

Harrisville Designs Shetland Style Wool (F/S): Woodsmoke

MULTICOLOR SEA DUCKS YARN LIST

(Each numbered item is the color, or color blend, used for an individual duck.)

Blues

1. Harrisville Designs 2-ply Tweed (W) in Lagoon Blue, with Harrisville Designs Shetland Style Wool (F/S) in Royal
2. Tipperary Tweed (B) N/A: teal green
3. Tipperary Tweed (B) N/A: teal blue
4. Harrisville Designs Shetland Style Wool (F/S) in Blueberry, with Halcyon Yarn Victorian 2-ply Wool (S) in #128 deep teal

Rusts/Reds

1. Tipperary Tweed (B) N/A: brick
2. Tipperary Tweed (B) N/A: maroon
3. Halcyon Yarn Victorian 2-ply Wool (S) in #114 brick, with Harrisville Designs Shetland Style Wool (F/S) in Garnet and Russet
4. Tipperary Tweed (B) N/A: red

Black/Charcoal

1. Harrisville Designs Shetland Style Tweed (F/S) in Ebony, with Halcyon Yarn Victorian 2-ply wool (S) in #134 black
2. Harrisville Designs Shetland Style Tweed (F/S) in Ebony, with Harrisville Designs Shetland Style Wool (F/S) in Navy
3. Harrisville Designs Shetland Style Wool (F/S): Aubergine, Navy, and Blackberry
4. Tipperary Tweed (B) N/A: charcoal

Grays

1. Harrisville Designs Shetland Style Wool (F/S) in Pearl, with Harrisville Designs Shetland Style Tweed (F/S) in Heath
2. Harrisville Designs Shetland Style Wool (F/S) in Pearl or Silver Mauve, with Jagger Spun 2/8 Maine Line Wool (F) in #8 Shale
3. A close-out medium wool tweed (S) in sage green, with Harrisville Designs Shetland Style Wool (F/S) in Pearl
4. Harrisville Designs Shetland Style Tweed (F/S) in Wildflower, with Harrisville Designs Shetland Style Wool (F/S) in Pearl

Border Linings

Choose a lightweight combination, e.g., sport weight Shetland Style, doubled.

GARDEN EXOTICA YARN LIST

Background

Harrisville Designs 2-ply Tweed (W): True Blue

Reds

Halcyon Yarn Victorian 2-ply Wool (S): #114 coral, #115 maroon, #138 magenta, #139 fuchsia, #141 red, #140 hot pink

Harrisville Designs Shetland Style Wool (F/S): Chianti, Garnet, Russet

Various novelty yarns with variations:
rainbow-dyed loopy mohair (W) N/A: reds/oranges/rusts/fuchsia
rainbow-dyed rayon/silk twist (W) N/A: reds/turquoise/gold/fuchsias

Halcyon Yarn 2/12 Pearl Silk (F): #6 Pale Ruby, #7 Rose Jade

Pink/Coral

Halcyon Yarn Victorian 2-ply Wool (S): #104 light coral, #113 medium coral, #111 dusty rose

Harrisville Designs Shetland Style Wool (F/S): Aster, Orange Peel, Apple Blossom

Reynolds Kitten wool/acrylic (W): #207 Pale Peach

Jagger Spun 2/8 Maine Line Wool (F): #26 Watermelon, #27 Apricot

novelty yarns:
loopy acrylic/rayon/cotton mix (S) N/A: beige/pink/coral
alpaca (S): soft pink
loopy mohair (W) N/A: orange/gold

Halcyon Yarn 10/2 Pearl cotton (F): pale and medium pinks

Halcyon Yarn 2/12 Pearl Silk (F): #7 Rose Jade

Vines

Halcyon Yarn Victorian 2-ply Wool (S): #145 sea green, #130 frosty sea green, #146 turquoise

Halcyon Yarn Mohair (W): #145 sea green, #146 turquoise, #130 frosty sea green, #131 sage

Harrisville Designs Shetland Style Wool (F/S): Peacock, Spruce, Juniper, Sea Green, Monet Blue (tweed)

FLORAL TAPESTRY YARN LIST

Reds
Halcyon Yarn Victorian 2-ply Wool (S) and Halcyon Yarn Mohair (W): #141 red, #114 brick, #117 garnet, #118 magenta
Harrisville Designs Shetland Style Wool (F/S): Red, Pumpkin, Topaz, Chianti, Garnet, Magenta

Oranges
Harrisville Designs Shetland Style Wool (F/S): Pumpkin, Butterscotch, Orange Peel, Coral
Halcyon Yarn Victorian 2-ply Wool (S): #141 red, #142 orange, #109 peach, #110 sienna

Greens—Main Leaf and Arabesques
Halcyon Yarn Victorian 2-ply Wool (S): #129 sea green, #130 frosty sea green, #131 sage, #145 jade
Harrisville Designs Shetland Style Wool (F/S) and Shetland Style Tweed (F/S): Dawn Mist, Peacock, Turquoise, Woodsmoke

Greens—Leaf Veins
Halcyon Yarn Taffy, 100% cotton (W): #31 pale sea foam
Halcyon Yarn Victorian 2-ply Wool (S): #130 frosty sea green
Harrisville Designs Shetland Style Wool (F/S): Sea Mist

Pinks—Pale
novelty rayon/acrylic blend (S) N/A: pale pinks/white/pale green
Harrisville Designs Shetland Style Wool (F/S): Apple Blossom, Aster, Lilac
alpaca yarn (S): pale rose
Jagger Spun 2/8 Maine Line Wool (F): #28 Rose, #64 Coral
Reynolds Kitten, wool/acrylic (W): #215 Deep Rose

Pinks—Dark
Halcyon Yarn Victorian 2-ply Wool (S) and Mohair (W): #138 magenta, #139 rose campion, #118 cerise

Dark Centers on Florals
Halcyon Yarn Victorian 2-ply Wool (S): #134 black
Harrisville Designs Shetland Style Wool (F/S): Aubergine, Iris, Garnet

Pale Orange on Red Flower
Halycon Yarn Victorian 2-ply Wool (S): #109 peach
1-ply silk/alpaca blend (S) N/A: coral
Harrisville Designs Shetland Style Tweed (F/S): Orange Peel, Pale Sherbet N/A

Dark Background Colors
Harrisville Designs 2-ply Tweed (W): Purple, Indigo, Black
Harrisville Designs Shetland Style Wool (F/S): Blackberry, Aubergine, Cobalt, Midnight Blue, Iris
Halcyon Yarn Victorian 2-ply Wool (S): #126 navy, #134 black

ORIENTAL MOTIF YARN LIST

Background Whites
Harrisville Designs 1-ply Tweed (F): Wild Flower
Harrisville Designs Shetland Style Wool (F/S): White, Pearl Sand
Halcyon Yarn Victorian 2-ply Wool (S): #103 white, #104 natural
Halcyon Yarn Mohair (W): #104 natural
Reynolds Kitten, wool/acrylic (W): beige

Various Skeins of Textured Yarns
thin cotton bouclé (F)—substitute Halcyon Yarn Ruffles & Lace, #30 off-white
silk/alpaca blend (S)—substitute Halcyon Yarn Snow Queen, #191 off-white

Corals
Halcyon Yarn Victorian 2-ply Wool (S): #113 dusty coral
Harrisville Designs Shetland Style Wool (F/S): Aster

Jade Green
Halcyon Yarn Victorian 2-ply Wool (S):
#130 jade

Blues
Harrisville Designs 2-ply Tweed (W):
Dawn Mist, Indigo, True Blue
Harrisville Designs Shetland Style Wool
(F/S): Loden Blue, Blueberry, Navy,
Cornflower
Halcyon Yarn Victorian 2-ply Wool (S):
#125 deep periwinkle, #126 navy, #128
deep teal blue
Halcyon Yarn Mohair (W): #125 deep
periwinkle

Lining for Borders
Halcyon Yarn Victorian 2-ply Wool (S):
#104 natural (knit singly)

FLORAL PATCHWORK YARN LIST

Background
Harrisville Designs Shetland Style Wool
(F/S): Cornflower Blue, Aqua Blue, Sea
Mist, Wedgwood, Silver Mauve, Pearl
Harrisville Designs Shetland Style Tweed
(F/S): Wildflower, Dawn Mist
Halcyon Yarn Victorian 2-ply Wool (S):
#122 lavender, #127 medium sky, #124 ice
blue, #130 pale aqua
Halcyon Yarn Mohair (W): #122 lavender,
#130 pale aqua, #124 ice blue
Jagger Spun 2/8 Maine Line Wool (F): #45
Cerulean, #46 Powder Blue, #37 Teal
Halcyon Yarn Scottish Tapestry Wool (B):
#126 pale baby blue, #127 medium sky
blue

Lily — Pale Pinks
Harrisville Designs Shetland Style Wool
(F/S): Apple Blossom
Jagger Spun 2/8 Maine Line Wool (F): #29
Petal Pink
Halcyon Yarn Victorian 2-ply Wool (S):
#112 pale dusty rose, #113 medium dusty
rose
Reynolds Kitten wool/acrylic (W): pale clear
pink

Halcyon Yarn 5/2 Pearl Cotton (F/S): #152
palest ice pink

Lily — Medium Pinks
Harrisville Designs Shetland Style Wool
(F/S): Peony, Aster
Halcyon Yarn Victorian 2-ply Wool (S):
#113 dusty rose, #116 muted cerise
Halcyon Yarn Mohair (W): #113 dusty rose

Lily — Dark Pinks
Harrisville Designs Shetland Style Wools
(F/S): Chianti, Peony, Magenta, Aster
Halcyon Yarn Victorian 2-ply Wool (S) and
Mohair (W): #140 bright pink
Halcyon Yarn 10/2 Pearl Cotton (F): #150
bright pink, #123 rose campion
cotton chenille (S) N/A: fuchsia

Greens for Stems, Leaves, and Borders
Harrisville Designs Shetland Style Wool
(F/S): Spruce, Hemlock, Fiddlehead,
Evergreen
Halcyon Yarn Victorian 2-ply Wool (S):
#128 deep teal, #132 moss green, #133
forest green
Halcyon Yarn Mohair (W): #144 bright
green
Halcyon Yarn 5/2 Pearl Cotton (F/S): #164
lime green

Oranges for Daylily and Poppy
Harrisville Designs Shetland Style Wool
(F/S): Pumpkin, Gold, Daisy, Coral
Harrisville Designs Shetland Style Tweed
(F/S): Orange Peel
Halcyon Yarn Victorian 2-ply Wool (S):
#109 peach, #142 orange
Jagger Spun 2/8 Maine Line Wool (F): #26
Watermelon, #27 Apricot, #63 Cassis
small bits of rainbow-dyed loopy mohair (B)
N/A
close-out wool tweed (F) N/A: pale orange/
beige/yellow tweed

Lily — Yellows
Halcyon Yarn Victorian 2-ply Wool (S):
#107 pale yellow, #143 bright yellow,
#108 medium yellow

Halcyon Yarn Mohair (W): #143 bright
yellow, #103 natural
Jagger Spun 2/8 Maine Line Wool (F): #23
Marigold, #24 Chrome, #25 Daffodil
Harrisville Designs Shetland Style Wool
(F/S): Cornsilk

Iris—Dark Purples
Harrisville Designs Shetland Style Wool
(F/S): Violet, Aubergine, Iris, True Blue
(Tweed)
Halcyon Yarn Victorian 2-ply Wool (S):
#123 smoky periwinkle, #148 purple,
#126 navy
Halcyon Yarn Mohair (W): #123 smoky
periwinkle
Reynolds Yarn Worsted Wool (W) N/A:
space-dyed in blues/navies/purples
cotton chenille (S) N/A: cobalt
Halcyon Yarn 5/2 Pearl Cotton (F/S): #126
purple, #157 cobalt

Iris—Pale Blues
Jagger Spun 2/8 Maine Line Wool (F): #44
French Blue, #45 Cerulean
Harrisville Designs Shetland Style Wool
(F/S): Cornflower
Halcyon Yarn Victorian 2-ply Wool (S):
#124 pale lavender blue

Poppy—Reds
Tipperary Tweed (B) N/A: red
Harrisville Designs Shetland Style Wool
(F/S): Red
Harrisville Designs Shetland Style Tweed
(F/S): Burgundy
Halcyon Yarn Victorian 2-ply Wool (S) and
Loopy Mohair (B): #141 bright red
Brown Sheep Wool/Mohair (W/B): claret

Poppy—Pale Reds
Harrisville Designs Shetland Style Wool
(F/S): Red, Coral, Pumpkin
Jagger Spun 2/8 Maine Line Wool (F): #26
Watermelon, #1 Cinnabar

Poppy—Maroons
Tipperary Tweed (B) N/A: dark maroon
Harrisville Designs Shetland Style and
Shetland Style Tweed (S): Garnet,
Burgundy
Pomfret Sport Wool (S): deep maroon
Halcyon Yarn Victorian 2-ply Wool: #117
garnet

Linings for Neckband and Lower Border
Jagger Spun 2/8 Maine Line Wool (F): #48
Cobalt, #55 Iris

Linings for Cuffs
Jagger Spun 2/8 Maine Line Wool (F): #32
Capri Green, #53 Turquoise